The Quest for Girthra

Mike:
Keep the dream Alive!

The Quest for Girthra

EPIC, HEROIC, MYTHIC, MYSTIC AND COMIC METHODS FOR CATCHING THE GREAT MUSKY

RICHARD A. MINICH

ISBN: 0-9758728-7-7

Library of Congress Control Number: 2004097534

All Esox Publications
P.O. Box 493
East Aurora, NY 14052

www.AllEsoxPublications.com

Original drawings by Laura Hahn
Copyediting by Steve McCabe
Editorial Services:
    Wordwright of Hamburg, NY (wordwright@prodigy.net)
Book design: Janice M. Phelps (www.janicephelps.com)

TABLE OF CONTENTS

ACKNOWLEDGMENTS

This book will probably ruffle some feathers, especially of the people who have put up with me these many years: my fishing partners, my club members, tackle suppliers, and residents of neighboring countries. Take it as it is: a satirical look at musky fishing, an attempt at finding truth through humor, or a sharing of my amusement at the quirkiness, odd behavior, and obsessions of the fanatical musky angler. It is an unusual man or woman who fishes the musky day after day.

Any similarity to people or organizations is purely unintentional. If I didn't love you guys, I'd ignore you altogether.

Richard A. Minich
July 2004

PART ONE

EPIC TALES OF MUSKY MEN

THE DREAM

"You've come to the right place, Finnegan, little buddy," said Commodore Gid. He'd come to meet his old friend and neighbor, Finnegan Mincher, on one of the "Straits Stretches" in the area around Pantherville. The Straits Stretches—Cormorant Island Pier, Finnegan Circle at Memory Park, Historic Towpath, Tiniwina Riverwalk, Swampherst Canalway, and other waterfront attractions—are various walking, biking, and rollerblading venues in the Straits Settlements, which is the local name for the cities and towns along the Musky Straits.

"How are you, you old nickel chiseler? Still clipping coupons?" Finn asked. His conversations with Gid were always a tableau. Gid sprinkled his part with proverbs that he used in the way Churchill used his cigar. Meanwhile, Finn's ball-breaking was an affectation of his, like Dean Martin's cocktail.

They shook hands. Gid was a handshaker, offering one up at the beginning and end of every meeting. Finn used handshakes more for emphasis than punctuation. They went with Gid's way. Only a boor declines an offered hand.

"Yep, still squeezing a buck 'til it screams," Gid said dryly, squeezing Finn's hand.

Finn Mincher smiled at hearing this. It confirmed at least one memory he had of Uncle Gid.

Finn had just returned to Pantherville after having spent 20 years working all over the world, most recently in the southern U.S. He'd run into Gilbert Ignatius David Gunmore the day before at an air show and had been astounded to see how young Uncle Gid had looked, as if the 20-year gap had never happened for him. They'd had no time to talk at the show and had agreed to meet on the Cormorant Island Pier for a walk the next day.

Just moments ago, Finn had parked his truck and walked toward the genuine 1943 U.S. Army Willys Jeep, which he knew had to be Uncle Gid's. Finn had neared the vehicle as he thought about his childhood and the old Uncle Gid. He had made out Gid's unique blocky stature, leaning against the fender of the Willys, as he had approached.

Gid Gunmore had always been a rare man on the straits. He was incredibly accomplished—mostly as an autodidact, a self-taught Renaissance man. He was tall, ruggedly handsome, and gave the impression of being square because of his massive shoulders and a flattop haircut.

Finn studied the man whose hand he was now shaking and saw that little had changed, apparently.

When Finn was a young man, he used to have unusual conversations with Uncle Gid. Gid was not really an uncle but preferred a less formal form of address than "Mr. Gunmore," and uncle seemed an adequate title. Those talks were part repartee, part instruction, part aphorism, and part vocabulary quiz.

The opening salvo in today's conversation certainly brought back fond memories. After a while, Gid spoke.

"If you want to learn about musky fishing, I can point you in the right direction." They had begun to walk to the pier.

"How did you know I was interested in finding out about musky fishing?" Finn asked.

"I have my sources," said Gunmore, smiling thinly and looking out over the straits as he continued.

"And I'm going to put you onto some sources that will help you understand what it's going to take, and what will happen to you physically, mentally, and psychologically, once you start."

Finn raised his eyebrows but said nothing. He wondered how Gid seemed to have been able to read exactly what was on his mind. Before he could say anything, Gid stopped and spoke quietly:

"If you like to catch a lot of fish, musky fishing is not the sport for you." He paused for a moment before continuing.

"If your first taste is too good, you will be sorely tried because it will not be easy again." He did not look at Finn as he spoke, and then he continued.

"Musky fishermen want their experiences to come with a bit of difficulty.

As Dr. Freud counseled, 'That which comes cheap is cheaply esteemed.'

Many a hammer is used up on the anvil of musky fishing."

Finn was getting his first taste of musky lore, but he knew these quotations were not original to Uncle Gid. He had heard some of them verbatim, or nearly so, many times before. But Gid was a man who could turn a phrase. He would take a complicated idea and reduce it to a nugget for Finn to roll in his palm and consider. Gid continued, pointing toward the water.

"There is a disgraced musky man right over there. His name is Terry Roberts—also called Yoda."

Finn looked at where Gid was pointing, toward a small man fishing on the rocks beside the pier. Finn agreed: Terry Roberts' expanding forehead, pointed chin, and gigantic ears did indeed make him look like the Star Wars character, Yoda.

"That may be your future if you persist in this musky hunting, Young Finn." Gid knew his interlocutor. He watched as Finn puffed up his chest, opened his eyes wide, apparently ready to accept any challenge and overcome it.

Gid went on, "Physically, a musky man consists of a bald head, a beer belly, and an overworked heart. The occasional thin one looks like a knot in a trotline, with bird legs accentuating the paunchy belly. Their hairless heads will have beards growing out of the ears, nostrils, and eyebrows."

Finn thought how age in men is disgusting, with hair growing in all the wrong places. Gid had once proposed a better system—one in which baldness started at the point of the chin and moved up. Many men would be happy to eliminate the slavery of shaving while keeping a little protection for the coconut.

"Unfortunately, as these musky men get old, whether from cigars or musky slime, or something else, they get a bit hircine—smelling of the he-goat," explained Gid.

"So," Finn thought, "our conversations will be like before: Gid just hit me with my first vocabulary lesson. I wonder what comes next?"

"I knew you'd build up my vocabulary, Uncle Gid," said Finn.

Gid smiled and handed Finn a few sheets of paper and said, "Here is the List of Forty Sayings of Musky Bill, which is the definitive Corpus of all you will ever know about musky fishing in the Musky Straits."

Finn took the sheets of paper from him as Gid continued, "Also, I'm giving you an item from my friend Otto Conrad that will give you a philosophic perspective on the journey you are about to begin."

Finn stammered, thought better of it, lifted his hand to make a point, dropped it, opened his mouth to speak, but finally closed it without a word. Again, Gid knew Finn would accept the passing of the baton, and he did.

They'd reached the part of the walkway that went under the Friendship Bridge over the straits. The shadow of the bridge caused a sudden coolness, which reminded Finn why it's always cooler by the lake in June.

Gid spoke again, "A lot has happened to the sport of musky fishing in the 20 years you've been traveling the world. I will be giving you additional handouts of the key items in the local lore—both original source material and secondary items."

They were back in the sun and walking upstream toward the lake. All the water of the huge lake seemed to be rushing toward them, as if it was coming down a chute.

"The lore of Musky Bill has been subject to constant study, criticism, and redaction over the years. It is told in five parts, following the endless troll of Melvin "Goober" Loonch and his various fishing partners and rivals. Some musky men take issue with some or all of Musky Bill's sayings. Some musky men say Bill is always right. But all musky men agree on one thing: the sayings of Musky Bill are *the* place to start if you are to learn about musky fishing."

Finn was trying to absorb all this when Gid continued.

"The knowledge includes epic and mythic tales, heroic deeds, and cosmic and ceremonial factors. Your path, guided by these materials, will take you to knowledge beyond measure. It will take you on a quest for the giant she-musky of myth, Girthra."

Gid pointed now to the sheets of paper Finn held before continuing. "Those innocent-appearing sheets of quotations compiled by Otto Conrad will affect you in indescribable ways."

Finn looked at the sheets he held: they sure didn't look like anything particularly profound. But he just nodded his assent anyway. He was having to take a lot that he was being told on faith. Gid continued.

"You will dream of mysterious things. Do not be alarmed." Gid spoke softly as they started back along the pier, walking with the current. Finn projected confidence and control in his persona—a survival mechanism from years of factory work—but in reality he had a childlike lack of guile that allowed Uncle Gid to pontificate without objection. He would at least hear Gid out and do his best to make sense of it later.

They walked together now to the end of the pier and gazed toward the water, a huge lake funneling into a mile-wide strait of visible current, and contemplated the vista silently for a few minutes. Then they started retracing their path back toward the vehicles.

"You'll notice the rat-like behavior of Yoda as we approach him again," Gid said. It was the first words that either had spoken since Gid had ended his advice to Finn with his warning. Gid went on. "He is known throughout the straits as a notorious preseason fishermen. He once tried to win an opening-day tournament in the Straits Musky Club with a fish that had spent several days in his live well. Yoda is one of the few left who feels the need to kill muskies."

Finn shook his head. He was a firm believer in catch and release. Gid went on.

"You must join the Straits Musky Club. The club is an important part of your quest. But it can be doctrinaire to an extreme and is also an obstacle to be transcended."

"But how can a club be both a help and a hindrance?" Finn asked.

"Because it is made up of men—competitive, striving, petty—all trying to convince themselves that they are the best fisherman and hoping also to make someone else notice." Gid continued while Finn stared.

"One strange tradition in the club is that board members tend to fall on their swords for the club about once per year. The most dramatic of these were Magnus Markson, Slim Tompkins, and Ike Borodino. It's something about being a man, being a musky man, anyway."

When Finn looked up, he noticed that they had returned to the parking area. Gid handed Finn a thin volume that Finn had not noticed Gid had been carrying on the walk. Finn now had three things to read. He glanced at the book and the papers Gid had handed him.

When he looked up, Uncle Gid and the Jeep were gone. Mincher couldn't understand the way time moved around Uncle Gid. He was confused as he looked at the first several typed sheets that Gid had handed him.

He read the first sheet, which was in list form, as follows.

MUSKY BILL'S LIST OF FORTY

1. There's no off-season in the straits
2. Musky fishing is a blood sport
3. No hair club for musky men
4. Fat guys to opposite sides
5. I'm a happy man
6. I wanna catch a big fish
7. A musky man even lies about his eels
8. We always get'em on the turn
9. Run, gun, and pound
10. The straits are the nurseries; the big fish are in the lake
11. Aren't we lucky to have this magnificent fishery
12. I'm a lucky man
13. Fish deep enough to get'm
14. Troll at three and a half up, down, or across
15. If you ain't cheatin', you ain't tryin'
16. Fish hard but smart
17. We could be out there right now
18. Be on the right spot at the right time; nothing else matters
19. If it works, do it again
20. It's great to be (not so) smart
21. {Ml = Mk + Mm} Musky lore equals Musky knowledge plus Musky myth
22. Real fish eat lures
23. I didn't catch any, but I lost a 50-incher
24. Remember what Flopp did on the Ottawa
25. Always use the hot color

26. Never eat a crème-filled cookie at sea
27. There's no such thing as musky music
28. Punt coverage rules apply on deck
29. Get to know plenty of Tonys, and you'll have a happy life
30. Ticklin' Tony is the only Tony
31. I could catch one right here
32. Tune your lures
33. Only orange bellies will work
34. Pinch their tails for a measurement
35. That Bogagrip is too short
36. Sharpen your hooks
37. Don't take a chance on old line
38. Only fish with someone you can count on
39. A musky hunter must be ceremonial
40. Whatever you've got, there's a musky that can defeat it!

Finn turned to the remaining single sheet of paper.
It contained the following.

Read The Epic of Gilgamesh *(pre-biblical creation story)*
1 Journey...
movement mirrors psychic change
...crossing the waters of death
...risking chaos...
primordial essence

You are embarking on an epic journey. Though you don't go far over the water, your spiritual journey will be great and dramatic. You will feel the power of heroism. And observe the misery of mediocrity—people who think like everyone else but not as effectively. Beware of the trap of Schadenfruede—joy at the distress of others.

The Duke of Wellington, when asked for words of advice when heading into battle, said, "Piss when you can." This is also appropriate for the musky man.

Otto Conrad

11

Introduction

GOMER AND GOOBER GO FOR GIRTHRA

Ian "Gomer" Draculitch and Melvin "Goober" Loonch are archetypal musky men. They are composites used to examine the famous sayings of *Esox* Guru Musky Bill. The tales feature many types of musky men. For your ability to imagine Gomer and Goober, here are their physical descriptions: Gomer is in his early fifties, wiry, spry, mechanical, tending toward neatness, and set in his ways. Goober is in his mid-fifties, thick set, tending toward fat, thick headed, sloppy, and reliant on the phrase, "That's why they call me Goober."

Study the List of Forty Sayings of Musky Bill in order to further your understanding of these anecdotes, which illustrate the epic, heroic, mythic, ceremonial, and Earth-shattering aspects of musky fishing.

Musky fishermen are seekers of truth; they come to the sport because their quarry is the most elusive of freshwater fish. She's the hardest to catch. She's the most unpredictable and solitary. She's also the largest of the freshwater fish normally considered game fish.

Most people start with the idea that hunting musky is a sport, such as golf or tennis, where in short order one learns most of everything one will ever know and spends the rest of the time refining one's skills in competition with other players. This is not so. There is no trunk full of musky knowledge wherein, once the key is found, one can sort through the lore and use it, to taste, like salt and pepper. There is a body of lore about musky fishing, but it is only a fragment of what there is to know.

Trophy musky are often caught by fishermen who are seeking other kinds of fish. Many guides and pros and experienced amateurs employ widely different methods that often seem mutually exclusive. If one goes to the waters that have a reputation for big muskies, one finds that the real experts have a great number of disagreements over techniques. Most acknowledge that they experiment from time to time to try to find new methods that will round out their knowledge.

When the Straits Musky Club was formed in 1994, the first meeting closely resembled a brawl over the subject of catch and release. Of the knowledgeable people at that first meeting, almost half wouldn't sign on to catch and release and reserved the right to kill their catch. This schism meant that half the knowledge of musky fishing on the straits walked away from the club. Those who left were the old guard, centered around Tank's Livery, where the heads of the water wolf were nailed to the wall in trophy fashion for years. Ten years after the founding of the Straits Musky Club, the top-twenty musky-killing contest has been gone for years.

Chapter One

PANTHERVILLE

There's No Off-Season in the Straits

The Musky Straits start in Pantherville and encompass a continuous band of towns and cities through Gunmore, Tiniwina, North Tiniwina, Whiteville, Cascades at the Strait, and, after the cataract, Palermo and Fortville. These villages span the area along the straits between the Upper Lake and the Lower Lake on the New York shore. When one takes into consideration the straits and the two lakes and their nearby feeder streams, there is no off-season for fishing. Trout, salmon, and various panfish are catchable all winter long if one is fishing in either the Upper or Lower lake or any of their immediate feeder streams.

Perch, a very popular small gamefish and table fare, has no off season. Walleye and Northern pike are out of season only during the month of April, when inland trout streams are open and legal. Only bass and muskies have a long restricted season: bass are only open from May through November and muskies from late June through November.

In the Lower Straits and the Lower Lake, some of the best luck is had during winter fishing, if one can brave the weather. During the winter, or, actually, when the water is below 40 degrees F., it is not unknown to catch one-hundred lake trout with one-hundred minnows. Lake trout have a short off-season and a slot limit, but brown trout and steelhead have no closed season in the lakes.

The Lower Straits don't freeze over because the ice is held back by an ice boom on the Upper Lake. With the Lower Lake dominating the fishing from December through May, all the other waters chip in some great angling the rest of the year, with tremendous smallmouth bass fishing, passable walleye fishing, and world-record-class musky angling in late fall.

One can catch grand slams and small slams in both the Upper Straits and the Lower Straits. In the lower straits, a grand slam consists of a Coho and a king salmon, and a brown, rainbow (steelhead), and lake trout, while a small slam need contain only two of the three trout species. In the upper straits, a grand slam is a smallmouth and a largemouth bass, a northern pike, and a muskellunge, while the small slam need contain only one of the species of bass.

Weather is the biggest detractor from fishing in the straits settlements. It is not seasonal weather changes that present the problem; it is the unpredictability of particular daily weather situations. Both spring and fall are subject to winds of such sustained force that it is life threatening to attempt to fish from a boat or even from shore. Winter, of course, has bad days, and even stretches of bad days, but there are also calm, temperate, sunny, windless days during the winter when fish can be caught near warm-water discharges and in other near-shore waters.

Summer has thunderstorms, when the waters should not be braved and only the foolhardy will venture out. All seasons have days of high, rushing water, when fishing is nearly impossible. While there is no off season, there are many off days in the straits.

Both the Upper Lake and the Lower Lake have areas contiguous to the Straits Settlements that have good fishing. Feeder streams that run ice-free during the winter and embayments near power plants are both available to residents and visitors to the Straits Settlements. A visitor to the area could catch a fish of a lifetime in the following species: Coho or king (Chinook) salmon, walleye, smallmouth bass, musky, catfish, rainbow trout (steelhead), brown trout, and lake trout.

Chapter Two

SOME OF THAT BLOOD COULD BE YOURS

SAYING NUMBER 2
Musky Fishing Is a Blood Sport

It isn't always the guy with the best reputation who puts a musky man onto the fish; sometimes inspiration comes from the oddest places.

Aunt Flo worked hard at using people to get what she wanted and had built her own hierarchy of people off of whom she preferred to sponge. If Gomer and Goober offered her a trip out fishing, she would go along, unless she got an offer from Johnny Lawrence, in which case she would stiff Gomer and Goober. If she was going with Johnny Lawrence and she got an offer from Bart Pilcher, then Johnny would be stiffed for the better offer from Bart. Only an offer to fish with legendary fishermen like Tom Westwood would be good enough for her to stiff Bart Pilcher. Gomer and Goober, being ignorant and silly, would rank below anybody in Aunt Flo's hierarchy.

The guy who catches a really big fish can be a newcomer or an occasional fisherman, like Hal "The Wallet" Goulash. In fact, it just so happened that Gomer and Goober broke their longest slump by following the advice of Hal Goulash.

The musky men use a channel on the VHF radio for keeping each other company. But, being competitive, they don't always include the lesser-known characters in their transmissions. It was easy to not answer a call from one whom they did not want to talk to by pretending the radio was off or out of order. This was usually what happened to Hal Goulash, and only a doofus like Goober would answer his calls. But Hal was the slump-buster as he hauled in the muskies at Schwartz Creek.

He called out one night to any member of the Straits Musky Club to tell of his fat fish, caught among the clouds of baitfish at Schwartz Creek. He said he had a 34-inch, 18-pound musky, which must have looked more like a beer barrel than a fish. Goober and Gomer headed down there for some of that action.

Draculitch and Loonch owed one to Hal Goulash. When they ran down to Schwartz Creek, they caught three suspended muskies trolling downstream after being in contact with Hal on the VHF. Downstream trolling is a bottom-contact method supposedly valid only in the mud-bottomed East Strait. Downstreaming in the rock-bottom West Strait is a non-starter. Downstreaming for suspended fish is doubly wrong.

So Goober and Gomer used a loser method on the advice of a knucklehead and broke their slump.

Later, as you learn of the sayings of Musky Bill, you will hear about Old Groaner and Girthra. Now, it's time to learn about some of the other subspecies of muskies. There is Growthra; there are the Boomers (Girthra wannabes) cruising the Lake depths; there are the Styrofoam muskies; and, most interesting of all, there are the war muskies.

First, a little background.

Musky fishing is all about size and danger, and the most sought musky is the giant she-musky of myth named Girthra. She exceeds 60 inches and 75 pounds and is as old as the hills. On the quest for Girthra, all kinds of muskies will be caught, and some of them are definitely the worse for wear.

Old Groaner was a legendary fighter that had survived having a sizable divot carved out of his side, blindness in one eye, multiple lamprey bites, as well as the ordinary trials of male musky life. In 1998 Goober caught a male named Growthra, and a month later he caught the same fish again. Growthra appeared to be an ordinary male except that under his chin grew a bony protuberance as big as a man's thumb. This growth jutting from below his jaw was red and raw and hard.

Let's examine the phenomenon of the war musky. The musky community is organized to protect Girthra, and one of its defense mechanisms is to send out the war muskies. Sometimes when an angler catches a small musky, that fish comes in like he doesn't even know that he's been hooked; he's easily unhooked and released with no fuss. This is a type of war musky known as the Styrofoam musky, and his mission is to put the angler off musky fishing by trying to convince him that it's really quite boring and not at all dangerous or exciting.

If the angler persists in trying to catch Girthra, then a different legion of the war muskies are sent in. These war muskies come in two varieties: the kamikaze and the ninja. Usually, the kamikazes are the smaller war muskies, and they are expendable. These fish want to get in your boat; throw the hook into one of your limbs; thrash and flop all over; slime your electronics; bleed everywhere; cause you an injury with hook, leader, tooth, or tail; or sink your boat and send you to sleep with the lawyers and zebra mussels at the bottom. Even a perfect release of a kamikaze war musky will result in some spot of blood appearing on your hand or arm where he got you and you didn't realize it. Simply put, the kamikaze war musky exists to inflict a hooking or worse injury on you.

So, Girthra's soldiers can come in as Styrofoam muskies to convince you the sport is no fun, Growthra, or other deformed muskies to scare you into worrying about catching something more than just a fish, kamikaze war muskies to bring the fight to you, and, if you still persist in trying to hunt down Girthra, the ninja war musky.

A little aside is needed about courage as it relates to musky fishing. People think that courage is rare in men, but the opposite is true. Most men are brave because they are embarrassed or ashamed to be otherwise. When a group of boys are together, they routinely dare each other to risk something, and the reason they do that thing is because the other boys are doing it. Courage is a social value. In the Civil War, the green troops who first went into battle had to "see the elephant" together to find out whether they would fight or flee. If everybody ran, there was no shame in running, but if one's mates stood and fought, it was incumbent on one to fight as well.

Musky fishing requires courage when the fish is landed, unhooked, and released. Ned Niawanda understands this fact and is a coward who makes sure he is always in a position where someone else will handle the fish when it is caught. This is usually done by freeloading on someone else's boat. To make up for this cowardice, Niawanda talks a big game, going on endlessly about his exploits. When the story is related to others, Ned takes on a heroic role that would make the uninformed believe that Niawanda is an old hand like Musky Bill.

Those who were in the actual boat at the time of the purported act of courage know that Niawanda was, in fact, prattling on in a nervous drivel, similar to a sportscaster, to cover his inadequacies. One tries to understand Niawanda's mind but can't fathom it. He is either thinking that the guy handling the fish believes Ned is the great heritor of Musky Bill or can't really notice that he is worthless and cowardly. Most people who fish with Ned Niawanda count on him for nothing more than holding a light in the dark.

But enough about courage; let's return to the adversary, the war musky.

The tactical doctrine of the Girthra defense forces is unknown, but it seems that the kamikazes that grow beyond the low forties in length become ninja war muskies. This is a rarer group than the kamikazes, and it is legendary. These are the fish that send boats adrift, pitch anglers overboard, leap into small boats with teeth flashing, reverse gaffs back at the fisherman, and perform other feats too prodigious to describe. Let's examine a recent classic encounter with a ninja.

Goober and Aunt Flo were out on a Friday night in August when the weeds were high, the water warm, and the muskies not biting. Then Aunt Flo got a big strike. One of the problems with fishing the straits in the summer is that the high weeds require very short lines. An angler might have only 50 feet of line out, sometimes even less. The boatman must make the musky pull against the boat because the current causes the boat to fall back on the fish immediately when upstream progress is stopped. This is a delicate maneuver because even a large musky can't pull a boat. On the other hand, too much slack line as the musky rushes the boat and the current drops the boat downstream would cause an increased risk of a lost fish. The combination of these two factors—short lines and falling back with the current—means the fish often isn't very tired when it comes to boatside.

Aunt Flo had hooked a very green musky, and it was a ninja. The first thing a ninja does is ram your boat. This generally does no harm, but it does demonstrate the courage of the ninja, and it is unnerving. This ramming can take place anywhere from five to 150 times. As one gets this fish near the boat and reaches for his front end to either gaff or Bogagrip the devil, he will either attempt to bite you, shake the hook into you, or take off on a mad, head- shaking dash toward another ramming run.

Aunt Flo's musky went around on these circular ramming runs about 15 times. He was never calm enough at boatside to be handled. A ninja has extra musky slime, as well, and the best outcome for the angler is a water release because the ninja wants to get that slime all up and down your boat. The other problem with the ninja's attempt to drag out the fight is the effect that it has of putting your battery on heavy discharge. If the boat has an inadequate electrical system, you could end up with a dead battery and a musky boat that is dead in the water.

That is what the ninja did to Melvin Loonch and Aunt Flo. The ninja never got in the boat, but he put two anglers out of commission, drifting toward the cascades at the straits, and therefore unable to hunt Girthra for the time being.

As you can imagine, the musky defense forces are formidable and relentless. It takes courage, stamina, and blood on the part of the musky hunter to continue the pursuit.

Chapter Three

I'M NOT ONLY THE SHADOW PRESIDENT

SAYING NUMBER 3

No Hair Club For Musky Men

Musky fishing represents a journey up the line to more difficult and time-consuming fishing. It is also a type of fishing that requires greater patience than the pursuit of smaller species. For these and other reasons, musky men tend to be older fishermen.

For the first few years that Goober and Gomer and Groovy fished for muskies together, they fished in Gomer's boat. This boat is 27 feet long and has a flying bridge over a hard top. The flying bridge is a great platform from which to photograph muskies and the men who catch them. Still photos are great; moving pictures are better.

Ian Draculitch and Bob Traynor both obtained video cameras. Draculitch uses his to take the odd musky movie, while Traynor shares his with his brother, Donnie. That means that whenever it is needed on *Mr.88*, Donnie's got it. Groovy Traynor's wife noticed something when reviewing the films of musky madness. Her discovery brought to mind the saying, "There is no hair club for musky men."

Since the fish are caught while trolling, they are almost always brought in from the back of the boat. This means that the filmmaker shoots from behind the angler, and bald spots show up in every frame. Groovy's wife suggested a special filter be added to the camera that would cover these shiny spots.

Musky men go bald in all sorts of ways. Gomer is the man with the amazing advancing forehead. Groovy has the Friar Tuck look just about completed. Goober was the first to succumb to baldness when he decided to forgo the swoophead look for the tennis ball effect of hair one-thirty-second of an inch long. By the way, Goober raves about having taken the maintenance of hair completely out of his life, allowing more time for fishing.

It isn't just the three Gs who have this hair-loss problem. Bart Pilcher's blond locks are disappearing like frog hair. Ike Borodino is the amazing colossal forehead.

As Christine Lavin writes, "You're not losing hair, you're gaining face." When Goober joined the fishing team, he had not seen Gomer for many years. Goober's first comment to Gomer was, "The last time I saw you, you had hair." Gomer's retort was, "Screw you."

It must be noted that these musky men have no problem growing hair in their ears or out of their nostrils. Their problem with hair-growing seems to exist only on their scalps. Some of the anglers in the Straits Musky Club have luxurious eyebrows that seem to have been growing unchecked for several decades.

Chapter Four

LET'S NOT MAKE A LIST

SAYING NUMBER 4

Fat Guys to Opposite Sides

If one has read any books or articles about the sea and ships, one knows the importance of weight distribution. Too much weight on one side of the boat can make it unstable. This instability can be caused by water in the bilge, ice in the rigging, or imprudent distribution of people.

Mr. 88 was anchored near a shore party one time when Ian Draculitch agreed to give the "kids" a little boat ride. It isn't normal for Gomer to be generous. While of a naturally pleasant disposition, he works hard to be tough and mercenary, believing survival requires this. Instead of three or four kids taking him up on his offer for a ride, he ended up with 17 people, including adults and teens. Against his better judgment, he lifted anchor and moved into the Upper Lake at the straits. Shortly thereafter, some kids got a little bored, then one yelled, "Hey, look at this," as he peered over the side of the boat.

With that, everyone ran for one side of the boat. Now, *Mr. 88* is a 27-foot boat, and it weighs 4 tons or more. It is normally very stable. But even this large boat needs balance. When all the kids crowded to one side, the stability of *Mr. 88* was threatened, and Gomer needed to get control of the situation by off-loading some passengers. Gomer returned to the shore party and hustled all his passengers ashore, regretting, once again, any show of humanity.

One of the problems with these aged musky men is weight. A lot of these guys are lardbombers, tubs, loads. Cy calls them "bombiedoloes." Maybe it is all the sitting, waiting for muskies to bite. Maybe it is all the time taken eating snacks. Something makes these guys broad in the beam, and that can cause Musky Bill to get upset over the way they move around in the boat.

Gomer and Goober spent three full days together in the St. Larry, fishing hard. At dinner on the last day, Gomer said, "I don't know how you do it. You don't eat any more than me."

"Less, actually," said Goober.

"But, how come you're so much bigger than me?" Gomer is sometimes bewildered by the variety of life. Goober goes about 220 and is stout through and through. Groovy goes from 270 to 300 and is apple shaped. Gomer, on the other hand, would probably weigh 160 if he had a brick in each of his back pockets.

With a reasonable number of people in *Mr. 88*, the shifting of people doesn't matter too much because the boat is well centered. The only time weight matters a lot is when Groovy stays in the back and drags down the speed at any given rpm. In *Booster*, a 25-foot boat without a hardtop, the weight distribution matters a lot. When it is just Goober and Groovy in the boat and Groovy is in a snit, which is about half the time, he won't come forward to sit in the cockpit when they are on the move to a new run. If big old Groovy stays way in the back, Goober can't see over the end of the boat. Groovy thinks he is Davy Crockett and was put on Earth to guide poor hopeless Goober in his bumbling fishing career. He therefore resists reasonable orders from the captain of the ship, Goober, expecting please and thank you instead of, "Bob, get your fat butt up here so I can drive!"

When Gomer drives *Booster*, an intricate ballet takes place as Goober and Groovy must keep on opposite sides of the boat, with only Goober cooperating in the movement. When Groovy is in one of his frequent huffs, he won't leave the back of the boat, and Goober can't sit in the co-pilot's seat because that causes listing to that side. Gomer says, "I don't mind. I'd rather be on the high side." Goober says it was Musky Bill who said, "Fat guys to opposite sides." Incidentally, there is no truth to the rumor that Sumo wrestlers have taken up the quest for Girthra after vacationing at the cascades at the straits. Nor is it so that Iggy is a Sumo wrestler.

Crab boats in the Bering Sea experience problems when ice builds up above the deck of the boat. The inherent danger of a top-heavy boat in those waters is obvious. If the bilge contains some water and the rigging is iced up, the boat may not spring back after a roll.

Gary Schreck is like ice in the rigging. Since he goes about 450 pounds, the boat tips with him when he moves from side to side. In *Mr. 88*, with its two inline six-cylinder engines, Gary Schreck can drop the speed by two or three miles per hour when he doesn't move to the front while the pilot is trying to get the boat up on plane. When on plane, a boat is traveling most efficiently because the smallest possible surface area is pushing water.

In *Booster*, Schreck causes two problems. As with *Mr.88*, he can hang out in the back and cause the boat to struggle getting up on plane. Gary also likes to hang his sizable butt over the same side that Goober is driving from. If Gary is hanging out behind Goober on the same side and the trolling run has them broached (sideways to the waves), it can become very uncomfortable for the boat owner. This is why Musky Bill says, "Fat guys to opposite sides."

All of this wouldn't be a problem if Schreck wasn't Pantherville's slowest individual. He always manages to find a few things to delay him, which gets the captain's teeth on edge.

Why not have Schreck drive and experience the problem firsthand? Goober tried that once when there were 6-foot waves. Gary waited until Goober was tending the starboard rod, then made a sharp turn broached to the wave. As *Booster* came down into the trough of an extra-large rogue wave, Goober found himself parallel to the water's surface and on the verge of being pitched overboard. It turns out that the best way to get cooperation from Schreck is to reference the List of Forty Sayings of Musky Bill, most of which Gary thinks he made up.

Chapter Five

'CAUSE MY STUFF IS BEST

SAYING NUMBER 5
I'm a Happy Man

(Happy is the man who reads aloud the List of Forty;
happy is the man who hears the sayings of Musky Bill)

One day, Stock Boy had some time to spend with Ian Draculitch while he did some small repairs to his boat. Gomer and Goober didn't know everything about musky fishing, but they were the archivists of the sayings of Musky Bill. While Gomer worked and Stock Boy helped, he asked about the saying, "I am a happy man."

"Anybody who dedicates his time and energy to musky fishing should be a happy man," Gomer had a gleam in his eye and a half-smile as he spoke and turned away. Stock Boy waited for him to say more.

After a while, Gomer went on.

"I'll tell you about that, but you have to understand a little about Goober and Groovy. They go back a long way and have been aggravating each other for decades. It seems as if Loonch is the only one who can get away with telling Traynor where to get off."

Gomer was adding power steering fluid to his starboard engine as Stock Boy held up the engine cover. Gomer went on.

"On the other hand, Groovy is a talking machine. He says the same things over and over as if you were deaf or dim-witted the first few times he's said it. The other thing about Groovy is that he has to one-up you. No matter what you've got, he always has the best of that type of thing, or he has a very close friend, who you are too screwed-up to know, who has the best and lets Groovy borrow it or play with it."

Gomer stood and screwed the cap down on the bottle of power steering fluid, and Stock Boy let the engine cover down as Gomer continued.

"Remember that during this time when he is one-upping you he is usually riding in your car or boat. Groovy Traynor doesn't own a house, has a crummy old car, has a boat that never gets wet, has no kids, generally has no job, has done no good works or any other kind of works, for that matter, and basically is a man in his forties with no resume at all."

Stock Boy laughed and shook his head. Gomer continued.

"A guy doesn't need to brag about his stuff because Groovy will jump all over it, comparing it to his or someone's that's better than yours. Well, since Goober and I have heard this stuff for years and years, we tend to ignore his blather, which has the unfortunate effect of encouraging him to repeat it."

"So, what do you do to shut him up?" Stock Boy asked.

"We don't," Gomer explained. "We treat the wind coming out of his mouth like the wind blowing through the boat's riggings—as background noise."

Stock boy shook his head and smiled as Gomer continued.

"One spring day, Traynor came aboard for some walleye or bass fishing, as musky season had not yet begun. We set off for the run up to the Upper Lake as a slight drizzle began. On this day, Bob Traynor's wife had recently purchased a new raincoat for him, and he started in with, 'I'm a happy man because I'm dry.' Then he'd tell us about some detail of the construction of the coat and say he was a happy man because the seams were waxed and triple stitched."

Gomer looked up before he went on.

"A little later he was a happy man because of the warranty on the coat. Then he was a happy man because of the way he didn't get too hot in his coat."

"Jesus, didn't anyone ever tell him to just shut up?" Stock Boy asked.

"No. There was no shutting him up," Gomer explained. "On and on he went until finally Goober had a meltdown and started asking Bob if he was a happy man every few seconds and saying he wished *he* could be a happy man. When Goober got to pounding Traynor with the happy-man stuff, Groovy got a bewildered look as if he didn't have any idea why Goober went over the edge that way."

"So he was clueless about how annoying he was?" Stock Boy asked.

"Totally," Gomer concluded.

Ever after, the phrase "I'm a happy man" became part of the lore of Musky Bill. Late one season, Goober did it to Gomer again. They were securing the boat and gathering their gear one evening about eleven o'clock. Stock Boy put a few things down for loading into Goober's car and headed over to his own vehicle. There, on the ground, was the bib overall part of a two-piece GoreTex foulweather suit.

This was a $250 outfit, of which all had heard many times what a happy man Groovy was since his wife had remembered him on his birthday. Apparently, he'd set stuff down to load into his car and had driven off, forgetting about half of his raingear.

"Hey Goobs, why don't you take that? You'll see him first." Gomer said. Goober turned the bibs over in his hands, studying their obvious quality.

"You know, Gom, I could use these up on the St. Larry." Goober began to get a strange gleam in his eyes as they headed home.

Later Goober told Stock Boy and Gomer that he had called up Groovy and the conversation had gone like this:

"Hello?" Groovy answered.

"I'm a happy man!"

"That's great, why?" Groovy asked, apparently clueless to the impending joke.

"Because I'm going to the cold northern reaches of the St. Larry in November to search for Girthra, and God dropped some great Gorky Park bibs in front of my truck last night," Goober explained.

"And it's really great, 'cause while I've got a good raincoat, I don't have a good set of authentic GoreTex rain bibs and slicker, and you know the weather might be rainy when we go to the St. Larry."

"No shit, where'd you find them?" Groovy interrupted. Ignoring this question, Goober went on.

"Yessir, I thought you'd want to know, I'm a happy man!"

"You want me to meet you someplace so I can get 'em?" Groovy asked. Goober continued to ignore him.

"I hear those fish up on the Larry are pinhead musky. That's why they claim a world record. Well, I knew you'd want to hear why I'm a happy man."

Goober hung up before Groovy could reply.

Of course, he eventually gave the bibs back to Groovy.

Chapter Six

WHY FISHING ISN'T GOLF

SAYING NUMBER 6

I Wanna Catch a Big Fish

Something that fishing and golf have in common is a tolerance for outlandish clothes. At least, it's supposed to be that way. Fishing is for relaxation, enjoyment of nature, comradeship, and contemplation—at least until the fish interrupts with a little excitement.

Ideally, fishing is noncompetitive except in the friendliest sort of way. Golf is all about betting and showing off and one-upping the other guy. Even goofy-looking golf clothes represent status in a backhand, cloistered sort of way.

In musky fishing, the boat locates the fish, the man lands the fish with rod and reel, and the team makes a healthy release. The least important person is the one who reels in the fish, and that job is usually given to a guest if there is one. Groovy Traynor likes to make that catching part into a saga of his prowess. In this respect, he is golf-like in his pursuit of celebrity status for the fish he has reeled in.

Golf is a great game. More people should golf.

Putting the lure in front of a musky ready to eat, or be aggravated into biting, is the most important and difficult part of musky fishing. By the time the musky makes the reel scream, she is hooked and will very often run toward the boat, which makes the reeling-in process fairly routine. If a fisherman can hold on for the wild ride that the musky usually gives getting to boatside, he can catch a musky. Measurement, photography, and release of the fish (also known as CPR, for catch, photo, release) is best done by a team to conserve precious seconds.

Apparently, none of this showcases the individual quite enough for Traynor.

Below Read the Testimony of a Musky Man

I know there are a great number of things about the musky that I will never know or only be able to guess at. For the past 4 years, my friends and I have fished hard for these brutes from late June until November, and we have improved each year. Yet we have a great deal to learn, for this is a mysterious creature that can confound all one's theories. The knowledge of musky fishing is esoteric and fuzzy, and even the old experts aren't too sure of everything.

The experts go out and get skunked on a fairly regular basis. It seems that when the knowledge of a subject is so nebulous, practitioners get very dogmatic in their thinking. They become wedded to their ideas and treat you as if it is your loss that your knowledge is so poor by comparison. This is because their facts can't be checked.

My hope is that, by admitting the thinness of my lore to myself, and that the ways of the musky are unknowable, I can retain my willingness to learn and improve my skills. For I have set my goal to be an expert musky man on the straits before I meet my maker. It is Girthra I am after.

End of Testimony

It started out that their fishing was for the fun of it. They would go after any kind of fish, mostly bass because they were easy and exciting. Usually, they fished the Upper Lake and sometimes even the Lower Lake or the Lower Straits. Weather sometimes drove them into the Upper Straits. It was all for a good time and relaxation, and they mainly took turns but never fought over fish for these fish weren't the event that muskies later became.

Late in the season one time, it got too rough for the Lake, and they ended up trolling for muskies on the river. Groovy caught one. It wasn't anything special—just 37 inches. Little did they know that the rout was on, and from then on the mantra was, "I wanna catch a big fish!"

Years have passed, and they have now become musky men in search of Girthra. When *Booster* was purchased, it didn't have a measuring stick for muskies. One had to be made. Goober decided to make it 60 inches long since he'd caught a 50-inch fish. It was therefore declared that if the fish is over 60 inches, one can claim any length. Ergo, $>60 = 100$ on *Booster*.

Chapter Seven

VIAGRA, ANYONE?

SAYING NUMBER 7

A Musky Man Even Lies about His Eels

Goober was trolling with Larry the Liberal when Larry mentioned the Jewish proverb that says time spent fishing is not considered time off one's life. Goober felt this to be a prescription for eternal life for him.

He thought about whether that made fishing the equivalent of jogging but without the pain. Goober had been doing a ratio delay study on joggers for years. (A ratio delay study is a series of random observations, which, when accumulated, give an idea of what percentage of the time someone is doing some act. For instance, if one drives by a swimming pool at random times in the summer, one begins to notice that the pool is almost always empty. A corresponding ratio delay study might indicate the pool was in use four times and the pool was idle 96 times to yield an estimate of 4 percent pool usage). He had yet to see one of these joggers who was smiling, and most appeared to be in agony.

The other thing about joggers is that they don't appear to need the exercise. One jogging woman near his home is so thin she appears to be disappearing up her own butt. Goober had seen these guys pounding their knees, dodging speeding vehicles, and inhaling exhaust fumes. Seven years of regular jogging adds 5 years to one's life, but the entire time is spent in pain.

Goober decided to stick with his butter, bacon, and french fries and hope that fishing would give him all the life he had coming.

"I've got another reason to be a happy man this year," said Goober.

"What's that?" asked Larry.

"I've got the opportunity to vote against Hillary this year."

"You know I'm a liberal," Larry replied.

"Yes, and I forgive you for it."

"I don't think Rudi can do anything for this part of the state. Hillary will bring a new perspective not dominated by the city," Larry countered.

"Yeah, the perspective of a doctrinaire socialist. This is Stalin with bad legs, and not quite so cuddly," Goober commented.

At this point, the conversation drifted away from politics.

Musky fishing, wherein one is untroubled by "tiddlers"— tiny fish of no consequence—is a contemplative pursuit that facilitates the maturing process of developing an inner life. There are long periods when one is working at musky fishing without reward or even encouragement. This is an almost perfect parallel to the working life of the average man.

At the same time, the rhythmic nature of musky fishing, from the waves, the wind, and the thrum of the motor, induces a semi-hypnotic state. In this state, the unconscious can slip past the guard dog of consciousness and occupy the mind.

Aunt Flo can be disturbing to this sense of solitude. She sings along with the radio, making up her own clever words, which are really not so clever when one has heard them many times. She constantly calls her sister Minnie to discuss every detail of her intensely trivial life. They call one another every few minutes and talk about what's for breakfast, getting a hairdo, or picking up the mail.

When she is not trying to drown out a better singer or calling her sister to report on nothing, Aunt Flo is laying out her stretchers. Goober has known Flo longer than anyone except his mother, but Flo still tries to impress Goober by telling big lies. If

Goober ignores the tall tales, they get piled higher and deeper. Goobs just goes on obliviously by pretending to be stupid in the head.

"Minnie has a new boyfriend. He's got two master's degrees, he's a pilot, and he's wealthier than anyone you know," Flo said. Money is a big motivation to Aunt Flo, especially money she doesn't have to earn.

She continued, "He's handsome, he's hip, and he's sophisticated."

Through Goober's mind races the thought, "What is he doing with Minnie?"

So, Aunt Flo went to Grandfather's Island for her vacation. When she returned, she began with the "I did this; I did that stories." She told of Cy and his wife coming up and catching the biggest striped bass of their lives. In the middle of this story, she made the claim that she even gets better bait than anyone else.

"I went to the bait shop and got some eels," Flo said. Sand eels are bait that are about 12 inches long. But Flo was holding her hands almost 2 feet apart as she told Goober about her better bait.

A thought jogged past Goober's mind that one of the List of Forty Sayings of Musky Bill was, "A musky man even lies about his eels." All men are concerned about length, and musky men perhaps doubly so. Aunt Flo must be a true musky man.

Boo, Coop, Otis, Lil' Reverend Dave, and Hoser were chatting at the marina.

"I'm going to get me some of that Viagra," said Hoser.

"Woo, woo, woo; going to be some screwin' tonight," Coop stated enthusiastically.

"I'd like to get hold of some anti-Viagra," said Boo.

"What's that?"

"Something to make the desire go away and stop bothering me," replied Boo.

"Here I am looking like a knot in a trotline, with my big boiler of a beer belly being 40 percent of my body, I've got coarse bristles growing from my ears, nose, and eyebrows but nothing on my head, my sagging butt no longer fills out my trousers, I smell like a billy goat, and can't imagine why any woman would be interested in me, but here's this little engine between my legs that thinks for itself and wants me to notice it all the time."

The other guys just looked at Boo, not understanding or sympathizing.

"In a matter of a few years, my self-image changed from Brad Pitt in *A River Runs through It* to Walter Matthau in *Grumpy Old Men*. Since there's no way I'm going to get back my youth, why be bothered by all these sexy thoughts."

Boo's remarks made it unlikely he was a musky man since he was unwilling to lie about his eels.

PART TWO

HEROIC MUSKY HUNTERS

DREAMING

Three weeks later, Finn met Captain Gid at the Historic Towpath in Pantherville for their next walk on the Straits Stretches. Gid arrived in an Opel and unfolded himself out of the tiny vehicle. Gunmore had a successful career as an engineer and was a tinkerer who loved new and unique equipment. He always had several vehicles. It would not have surprised Finn if Gid had driven up in a Conestoga wagon.

Finnegan Mincher had a number of questions about the *Epic Tales of Musky Men*. He also wanted to control the conversation a little more this time. The two men headed up the Historic Towpath, and Captain Gid pointed out the notorious musky killer, Mel Dumke, by rolling his eyes in the direction of the snack bar. Dumke had gone over the edge one day, declaring that he hated muskies, hated the Straits Musky Club, hated the board of directors of the club, and would kill every musky he saw from then on.

Upon hearing this, Bart Pilcher, worm magnate, had said, in an aside to Snooky, "That won't harm many."

On this day, Dumke stood rooted in front of Oat Willie's hot dog stand. The two workers inside were pinned down by a stream of elaborate hogwash.

Dumke had been evicted from his girlfriend's house and was living out of a Buick. He spent the day pestering anyone who came down to enjoy the towpath. Dumke is a witling. He thinks he's funny but he's not. He tells foul jokes, stupid jokes, dirty jokes, but specializes in anti-Catholic jokes. They are so embarrassing to hear that he's been seen at musky meetings chasing people around trying to finish one of his involved stories about nuns while they try to get away from him.

Mel Dumke is typical of Pantherville because he is so odd. Viewed from any angle, his head appears to be an upside-down pyramid. From the front or back, the base is the top, and from the sides the back appears flat. This carved head accentuates his nose and makes him always seem to be looming toward anyone in conversation with him.

The infinite ethnic variety within the Straits Settlements, shaken and stirred, produces oddities like Mel Dumke. He has a pencil neck, a pointy nose, high cheekbones, a pointed chin, and eyes that are too close together. Dumke would be useful if, while working on a stepladder, one needed a flat place to hold small parts. The top of his head would serve the purpose well.

In addition to his look of a half-baked mongrel dog, he's a *goobermensch*—a guy who thinks he's really cool but isn't cool at all. Mel Dumke bought Bart Pilcher's old boat, the *Stinker*, and promptly ran it aground on Scull Reef. He fancies himself a fishing expert and a charter captain, but he had bought an undersized starter boat and failed to remember where the cut through Scull Reef was. He is a joke in the straits.

Captain Gid and Finn avoided Dumke by quick footwork and walked down the towpath. Finn shook his head in wonder. Gid had imparted all that knowledge about Dumke with just a nod, a wink, and a slight rubbing of the chin. He hadn't said a word.

A walk along the towpath passes many people fishing from shore, catching and keeping small fish of any kind. Finn asked, "In your *Epic Tales of Musky Men*, do you address dreaming? I've been having some strange dreams, some about muskies, many not."

Gid paused for a moment, then looked up as he spoke.

"The tales generated to explain the List of Forty are not mine; they are the tribal wisdom of a hundred years distilled through Musky Bill." Gid paused before changing the subject as he continued.

"I'm not an expert at dream interpretation, but I can tell you that it is the page of notes from Otto Conrad that triggers that dreaming. He just gives suggestions that unleash a stream of thoughts from the unconscious. These are collective memory and individual experiences melded by your recent activities and told in a story of words and images. As you move along in your exploration of musky lore, your dreaming will intensify and begin to occupy more and more of your waking life."

Finn raised his eyebrows and nodded as he absorbed this, then spoke.

"So, how do I know when and where to meet you, since we don't set a date? Is that a dream message?"

They were about halfway to Tank's Livery, a famous spot for meetings of the musky men in the days before catch and release. Gid sat on a bench and Finn joined him, awaiting a reply to his questions. Boats roared by on the straits heading for the Upper Lake to the south. Many were sizable booze cruisers that would have no problem with the 5- to 8-foot waves predicted on the lake that day. Johnny Lawrence came past with his huge musky net stuck up like a flag. Johnny chartered out of a 17-foot open boat that was little more than a glorified flat-bottomed bass boat.

"I don't think I would brave 8-footers in that boat," said Mincher. Gid ignored this comment and replied instead to the original questions posed.

"Musky fishing is like baseball: getting home safely is what counts," said Captain Gid.

Mincher and Gunmore began walking again.

"Last night, I had an odd dream that seems more real now than my memories of the last few days," Finn offered.

"Mm-hmm."

Finn took this as his cue to begin.

"I was taking my dog for a walk, leaving from my home in East Arundel, but in a Datsun pickup I owned 20 years ago in Ohio. I headed up a mountain that I had worked near in West Virginia 15 years ago. The dog, my wife's dog, Alex, was in the bed of the truck. She hated that, was always afraid he'd jump out, but up the mountain we went." Gid nodded and Finn continued.

"Next, I'm letting the dog run free over the strip-mine spoil banks in Ohio. They are almost straight up and down. The dog spotted a bear and took off after it, out of sight, almost immediately, over a ridge. I went after him, up and down. The joke in those parts was that most guys had one leg shorter than the other from running the ridge tops. I called, climbed, came down, went up, filling my boots with gravel from the spoil banks. The dog and the bear easily outdistanced me." Finn looked up to see Gid rubbing his chin as he listened. Finn went on.

"Then the dream fast-forwards to me and Alex back at the pickup with a dead bear in the truck bed. How we got there I don't know. I drove down the mountain with the dog on the seat beside me. At the base of the mountain, the road came to a fork. There was a small country store with a dozen kids playing around out front.

'Well boy, let's see what they think of your bear,' I said to Alex and got out of the truck. The kids were all crowding around, staring. I turned to show off my bear, but when I looked there was nothing in the pickup bed. But draped across the top of the cab was a Pantherville football player, in uniform, who was famous for his sleep apnea. One of the children said, 'Oh, sleeping.'"

Finn paused for a moment before concluding, "What kind of a dream is that?"

Gid pursed his lips before replying. "I'm no expert on dreaming, but Otto has told me some things. All that climbing and descending is symbolic of the sex act, or several acts, in this case. Time condensation and distance compression are common in dreams, and you were obviously feeling guilty about endangering the life of your wife's dog and temporarily losing him."

Gid looked up at Finn and spoke, "Beyond that, I can't say."

They rounded a corner, and there was Tank's Livery, with a

faded top-twenty board still hanging on one wall. The names Horace Ball, Ike Borodino, Slim Tompkins, Marcus Quimby, Don Maynard, Ernie Ochefski, Magnus Markson, Tom Westwood, and Don Enkadu were all up there. Some names were repeated two or more times on the board. Finn studied the faded list for a few minutes, then looked down at his hand.

He had a new sheet from Otto Conrad and another slim volume in his hand, but he had no recollection of having received either. Though they had walked 2 miles down the towpath from where they had parked, Gid Gunmore had vanished.

"Of all the tyrannies, a tyranny exercised for the good of its victims may be the most oppressive. It may be better to live under robber barons than under omnipotent moral busybodies. The robber baron's cruelty may sometimes sleep, his cupidity may at some point be satiated; but those who torment us for our own good will torment us without end for they do so with the approval of their own conscience."
C.S. Lewis

"We shall practice revenge and outrage against all who are not as we are."
Zarathustra

"Ritual is symbolic behavior consciously performed. It is the use of the faculties like dreaming that enables us to set up a flow of communication between the conscious mind and the unconscious. Our institutional hunger for meaningful ritual stays with us today, even though we have lost our sense of the psychological and spiritual role in our lives."
C. Jung

"Jody lay in his bed and thought of the impossible world of... a world that ceased to be forever. He wished he could have been living in the heroic time, but he knew he was not of heroic timber. No one living was worthy to do the things that had been done. A race of Giants had lived then, fearless men, men of staunchness unknown in this day."
John Steinbeck"The Leader of the People"
The Long Valley

*2. Hero...superior man...represents... strong...handsome...wise
3. Embodiment of moral virtue*

Otto Conrad

INTRODUCTION

It started a couple of years ago when Bob "Groovy" Traynor was unemployed and spent all day at tackle shops picking up lore but mostly telling stories about himself. He would come to the regular weekly fishing trip on Gomer's boat, *Mr. 88,* and rattle on like a milk jug with 50 pennies in it.

Bert Pilcher's Hunting, Fishing, Poaching, and Cheating was the store where Groovy got much of his information. He'd say, "Bert said, 'You can't catch them there,' Bert uses Xpost Facto rods, Bert fishes there in the fall, or Bert likes a hot color." Bert this, Bert that—Groovy would drive everyone crazy with his incessant blather about Bert.

Traynor got to working Bert hard for musky lore, and when Traynor latches onto someone, he is good at what he does. Everyone knows what it's like to listen to someone who goes on and on.

There are only a few reasons why one's supposed friend would subject one to such incessant drivel: he thinks you are so screwed up you don't know anything and can't remember what he has told you 50 times, including three times in the last 15 minutes; he's truly malicious and is genuinely trying to tick you off; he's so insecure he needs to keep reassuring himself that he's more adequate than you; or he has truly convinced himself that he's helping you with his constant instructions. Possibly, that is all there is to the guy: three repetitions of the latest drivel to occupy his pea brain.

Anyway, Bert Pilcher, worm salesman, outdoorsman, and musky guide, became topic number one with Traynor that summer. Goober became convinced that Traynor would go out on the weekly fishing trips on *Mr. 88* just so he could then go to the tackle shop the next day and get Bert's perspective and criticism on everything that had transpired, while having a good laugh at the stupidity and ineptitude of Gomer and Goober, his supposed buddies.

The next time the three went out, it was "Bert this, and Bert that" again. Well, lo and behold, Bert did have some good ideas and some tackle products that enhanced the fishing experience. Since some of his ideas worked when tried, it got to be a regular feature from Groovy, called "The Bert Report," as they pulled away from the dock to strain the water.

Goober, being an iconoclast of the first order, began to egg-on Traynor by asking stupid questions and repeating stuff until Groovy got flustered. Then Goober would start calling Bert "Bart" and using his name in a lot of sentences and repeating Bart every time after "Bert" was said by other people. Goober can get very exasperating when he does this, although it can be hilariously funny as well. So "Bert" became "Bart" and would remain so thereafter on the fleet in search of Girthra.

Bob Traynor is a big guy built like an apple on stilts. As such, he is ungainly in a boat, tending to unbalance the boat to whichever side he is on. Even in port, he is like a Hippo on roller skates. His build also makes it difficult for him to keep his pants up, which may explain why his pockets always seem too low for him to contribute to expenses.

Bob's problem is that he's a trust-fund baby. He never had to work. He never had to slay his own dragons. He's afraid of a physical challenge, afraid to make a decision that may be wrong.

Traynor is a charming guy with the gift of gab but is also a perpetual adolescent. When one first meets him, there is an initial infatuation, then the sayings and manipulations wear a little thin and one begins to recognize the limitations of his repertoire and his thinking: the same jokes, the same sayings, the same prejudices. Then, finally, his blather becomes just like road noise—easily ignored and not upsetting. One comes to the realization that he can't help it.

Chapter One

HOW EDDIE GOT HIS RUN

SAYINGS NUMBER 8 AND 9

We Always Get 'em on the Turn/Run, Gun, and Pound

The reason they are called Gomer and Goober is because of the crap they took from Groovy. Nicknames and musky slang are a part of the straits musky scene. Some nicknames are affectionate, some are respectful, some are put-downs, some are made up by the named person to prevent a putdown, and some are the radio handles of the musky men.

Gomer and Goober fished with Groovy for years on Gomer's boat. They made the journey up the line together from general fishermen to musky specialists. Over the time this was happening, Bob Traynor spent more and more time and effort absorbing lore from some of the more accomplished musky men, like Bart Pilcher, Tom Westwood, Slim Tomkins, Don Maynard, and Johnny Lawrence.

Dale Carnegie teaches us that to make a person like you, one should show an interest in his favorite subject. That subject is, invariably, himself. Groovy is very accomplished at this technique. In the short run and in small doses, he seems eminently charming, witty, and personable. Everyone has heard about people who are gifted. A person can be gifted athletically, musically, artistically, physically, and intellectually. Bob "Groovy" Traynor is gifted socially.

He can turn his charm on in a second with what seems like no effort at all. He feels no embarrassment at spouting the same clichés and platitudes, which somehow always sound just right coming from him but would be perceived as hopelessly stilted and contrived coming from anyone else. This capability puts strangers at ease and is the social gift that lubricates Groovy's passage through life. However, one who has known Groovy all his life will tell you that bullshit is all that there is.

Knowing Groovy is like the existentialist nightmare wherein the philosopher unmasks reality only to find another mask and then just more masks all the way down. Since Traynor's agenda is to get every personal advantage he can from others as he moves through life, he is obsessive in his obsequiousness to those who have the most to offer him.

Thus, it came to pass that Gomer and Goober could no longer do anything right in the eyes of Groovy. He had learned from Bart, Slim, and Johnny Lawrence many of the secrets of trolling the straits. Rather than tell Gomer and Goober what Bart or someone had said, he began to simply snort and shake his head and roll his eyes at their methods—presumably so that when he met Bart at the Tackle Shack, he could have a good laugh at how stupid Gomer and Goober were.

When asked to comment at the time as to when and how the boys should fish, he invariably said, "I'm easy," meaning he wasn't going to venture an opinion. This is classic passive aggressive behavior: if he didn't offer anything constructive, he could feel free to criticize Gomer and Goober to his buddies at the Sport Shop. When Goober got his own boat and had a few rough spots in handling it, Groovy went through facial contortions, laughed out loud, and engaged in other histrionics as docking and other maneuvers were learned. Since Gomer and Goober were so clunky in their approach to musky fishing, they gave themselves the Gomer and Goober nicknames to poke fun at the situation.

Gomer's boat is quite a bit larger than most of the musky boats on the straits. As such, it has earned the role that the traffic on the straits takes its cue from *Mr. 88*. Gomer is not able to change course with the nonchalance of smaller boats because, as the role-model big boat, everyone would change their course based on what he had done with *Mr. 88*. Because of the law of gross tonnage, which states that the more maneuverable boat must give way to the less maneuverable boat, smaller boats can alter course without notice. Bart trolls downstream on the straits in a zig-zag pattern, which is difficult for larger boats to do. Bart puts his boat in neutral to reel in his lines. If this were done by *Mr. 88*, it would again disrupt traffic as the boat everyone is reacting to would be slewed sideways down the river.

Groovy is very interested in his equipment, which we know is better than anyone else's, but seldom shows any care for the most important piece of equipment: the boat in which he is fishing. He will put the boat in neutral and walk away to check his rod while the boat loses way and begins to broach. Goober claims that one time Groovy almost pitched him out of his own boat when he turned sideways to a 7-foot wave and simultaneously rushed to the same side of the boat as Goober.

Because of the differences in boats, the approach to trolling the straits used by Gomer and Goober in their boats, *Mr. 88* and *Booster*, is more continuous than that of Bart and some of Groovy's other friends. Large boats can't slip into neutral and drift, except for a fish. If they wallowed around everytime Groovy wanted to change his lure, the wind would get hold of their high profile and the waves or current would turn them sideways.

Gomer and Goober fish Bart's Rip, the Pentangle, Frog Creek, the Graveyard, White Creek, Honey's Hole, and the Chrysler Run, which are all noted hot spots on the Upper Strait. They also have claimed Herbie's Hole, Sideby Strand, Mickey's Run, the Drumlins, and Eddie's Run as their own discoveries. But while Gomer is piloting his boat on a continuous loop that includes a number of the above spots, the little boats buzz around like bees at the hive as they run, gun, and pound their favorite spots.

One time, Gomer and Goober trolled down toward what is considered the start of the Chrysler Run. When they were about 200 yards from the place where one turns across the river, Bart's 19-foot boat came zooming by, too close for comfort, pulled up in front of them, and started across the run. In short order, two of Bart's mob came along in their boats and did the same thing. Each one got a little closer to Gomer and Goober and cut them off a little more and defied the rules of the road a bit more flagrantly than the last. Apparently, they had to pound their run and then gun to the next one to follow the sayings of Musky Bill. Bob Sapphire once was so intent on turning out at the exact end of the run that he didn't even look to his left as a cruiser came upriver at 30 mph. That made for some interesting radio chatter.

Groovy lobbied for the Chrysler Run often when he was in Gomer's or Goober's boat, and, as the cross-river part of the run was about to end, he would say, "We always get'm on the turn."

Gomer's comment was, "We must be true followers of Musky Bill because on the endless troll we never stop turning."

Gomer uses his boat for business in the sense that he takes out associates to repay favors. He takes out Otis, Floyd, the boys from the Noco station, and others. Each year, he takes Artie Breadcrumbs for an evening of fishing. Artie got his nickname by leaving trail mix all over the place when he had gone out one time. When men go fishing, they usually exercise their independence from their wives with a few beers and some junk food snacks. They do things they'd get yelled at for doing at home.

Though Gomer and Goober are both occasional beer drinkers, they usually stick to diet soft drinks while fishing. One recent season, Artie brought his friend Eddie along for some fishing. No sooner had the boat left the marina than Eddie went to the back deck, knelt down, and began a series of what appeared to be prayers and incantations. Gomer and Goober looked at each other quizzically and thought no more about it.

As the night wore on and Artie and Eddie had a few beers, they began to consume prodigious amounts of snacks, including an entire quart jar of pepperoncini hot peppers. Each beer and batch of peppers led to more odd behavior from Eddie, including dancing, shouting from the flying bridge, and weird rituals with the spare rods. Eddie seemed to fit the category of harmless eccentric.

It was the next time Gomer and Goober went out that they actually talked of Eddie while trying out a new run. While invoking the mantra of "Ed-dee, Ed-dee," the boys landed four male muskies of 36, 37, 38, and 40 inches. Ergo, the new hot spot was dubbed Eddie's Run.

A year later, Eddie's Run would be the top off-peak hotspot that would demonstrate the "run, gun, and pound" approach. What most local musky anglers recommend is downstream bottom-bouncing in daylight early in the season. They don't mean going straight downstream, which is exactly what Goober did on Eddie's Run, but using a zig-zag approach. Gomer and Goober would run downstream for about 15 minutes, gun back to the start, and pound the run over and over.

Sometimes it took eight runs to get the fish to bite, but bite they would. Often, in the east branch of the Musky Straits, the fish are there, but conditions bode ill for a successful presentation. If you can find a presentation that will work and you can make it happen amidst the boat traffic, you've got something as good as Eddie's Run.

Chapter Two

THE SIZABLE SEVEN

SAYINGS NUMBER 10, 11, AND 12

The Straits are the Nurseries; the Big Fish are in the Lake/
Aren't We lucky to Have this Magnificent Fishery/
I'm a lucky man

When the Straits Musky Club was born, it was born of controversy over catch and release. During its early political phase, it threw out one of the top musky men on the straits, Magnus Markson. The politics revolved around how much information is given out to those who need it, in or out of the club.

Magnus Markson is a man of renown in the musky-fishing world. He knows where to fish, but he ain't tellin'. There's a word for the information Magnus Markson has passed on to the club: it's "nullibiquitous," or "not existing anywhere."

The Straits Musky Club likes to support the fishery but would like to do so by closing the door behind themselves and not publicizing the fishery. The club wants to help non-musky fishermen handle their accidental musky catches to the musky's best advantage. When the releases began to be tallied, Magnus Markson was the man to keep the data. It was supposed that the club members could share their data and learn to be better fishermen. Though he inevitably caught the biggest tournament fish, Magnus Markson shared no data. His years of experience were not going to be given away. He would enter one fish in a contest, and that fish would be the winner by one-half inch over everyone else's. The irony of the fact that Markson was able to out-lie a bunch of liars went unappreciated by most.

The sizable seven were a group of Straits Musky Club members who took umbrage at Magnus winning a tournament by half an inch. Bob Traynor, Johnny Lawrence, Slim Tomkins, Bert Pilcher, Benson, Ike Borodino, and Tom Booker went to the board and demanded a change in behavior by Magnus. Magnus panicked, and instead of just denying all the charges that had been laid against him, he just quit the club. The sizable seven were vindicated, although they forgot that they, too, might have transgressed against the stated aims of the club with things like preseason catches, disturbing spawning habitat, and other less-egregious violations.

Markson still catches a lot of fish despite being out of the club. He was the man to realize that "the straits are the nursery; the big fish are in the lake." He writes articles and achieves modest notoriety by keeping the location of his angling successes quiet. "Aren't we lucky to have this magnificent fishery," is the motto of Magnus Markson. He doesn't give anything away to the Ohio boys or the Pennsylvanians. One of his magazine articles showed the same fish held by several different fishermen and presented each time as a different fish.

Bob Traynor likes to use the phrase, "I'm a lucky man," whenever he catches a big fish or his first fish of the day. Usually, the boys take turns on *Mr. 88* or *Booster*. That system is not good enough for Traynor, since he has better equipment and skill: he always wants to fish his own rod. That's the way Bart does it on his boat. On *Mr.88* or *Booster*, the last man to catch a fish goes to the center rod. The center rod is usually the least likely to strike a fish, but it is not always that way.

One summer evening, Bob was fishing one of Manny Jondier's famous lures and caught a 35.5-incher. He was then moved to the middle position and caught a 36.5-incher. He stayed in the middle and caught a 38-incher. He was a lucky man and had the right lure.

Editor's note: Magnus Markson is still at it, but now he uses **The Straits Shooter** *(a local newspaper) to get his gloss and still manages to gain one-half inch on his competition, Johnny Lawrence. As one season came to a close at the end of November, it was a competition between Magnus and Johnny to see who could get better mention in the paper. They enhance their chances by plying the writers with liquor and taking them out on trophy-fishing adventures. Markson recorded a 53-incher, Lawrence got two 53.5s, then a 53.75 (all these were charter fish, attributed to customers) before Magnus Markson edged everyone by his customary half inch with a 54.25-incher.*

Chapter Three

THE ENDLESS TROLL

SAYINGS NUMBER 13 AND 14

Fish Deep Enough to Get 'em/Troll at
Three and a Half Up, Down, or Across

Time went on and Groovy Traynor became more insistent that everything had to be done Bart's way. Gomer and Goober largely ignored him. It came to pass that Groovy began to learn conflicting facts from Slim Tomkins, Manny Jondier, Johnny Lawrence, and Tom Westwood. Everyone doubted Musky Bill's Saying Number 14: "Troll at 3.5 mph up, down, or across."

The straits behave like a river—with current, back eddies, slow spots, and necks where the current speed increases. Manny Jondier only trolls downstream, and he always goes very slowly, maybe 2 mph. Slim Tomkins goes as fast as 5 mph. Johnny Lawrence uses a different speed up and across than he uses downstream. These are expert straits musky men, and they do not always follow the sayings of Musky Bill.

When Goober got his boat, *Booster*, it was late in the boating season. The boat had an old and inferior depth finder and no speedometer. Gomer and Goober decided they were going fast enough by the action of their lures. In fact, different lures react better to different speeds. In order to explain this, I'll have to use some technical mechanic-talk.

"Hey Goober, can you bump it up just a chin whisker," Gomer said, watching his lure in the water.

Goober, being Goober, hit the throttle a little hard and had to back it down, then up, then down, while watching the tachometer with one eye.

"How's that, Gom?"

"Back it down just a chin whisker."

This would go on for a few minutes, until Gomer was satisfied, at which point they'd be about back where they had begun. This was entirely too inaccurate a method of speed control for Traynor, and he pointed out that Bart, observing from his boat, had felt Goober was going too fast. Oddly enough, the speed employed was able to catch fish, and, until Traynor caught a 36-incher, nothing under 40 inches had been caught with the tachometer-and-chin-whisker method.

Goober's boat had another big problem: its depth finder. As a straight bottom-finder, it sort of worked. However, when someone tried to activate the additional features that it supposedly had, it got a headache and spewed outlandish and contradictory data. It was only after Groovy attempted to fix it that it had one of these seizures, right in the middle of the Chrysler Run. When Groovy asked, "What's the depth?" Goober said, "Don't know."

"Come on, what's the depth? I need to know how far to let out my line."

"Don't know. I turned it off. It's meditating."

"For Christ's sake, I gotta know the depth." Traynor pulled in his line and refused to fish until Goober decided that the headache to his depth finder was gone. At this point, Goober put out a second line on Groovy's corner and the thought first occurred to him to advertise the corner for rent by season or trip.

Lures run at different depths. The amount of line out makes a difference. The type of line also makes a difference. The lure might be reputed to run at 20 feet yet not hit bottom in 13 feet of water. Muskies inhabit all depths. Muskies can swim. Muskies are three or four feet long and can lie in one spot like submarines. Muskies can also move like whips, faster than the eye can see. Depth finders are nice and helpful, but when fishing familiar runs they are merely anecdotal as long as you "fish deep enough to get 'em."

A recent article in the Straits Musky Club newsletter described perfectly the endless troll employed by Goober and Gomer: one trolls downstream in the spring, runs figure-eight patterns until trolling upstream in the summer, and then does figure-eights until the fall, when one again trolls downstream.

Chapter Four

WHO WAS THAT MASKED MAN?

SAYING NUMBER 15
If You Ain't Cheatin', You Ain't Tryin'

Fishermen stretch the truth, and fishing tournaments are built around this fact. Fishermen will go to great lengths to win. At one point, Goober was really screwing Yoda up; he wouldn't join his club, and a non-club-member couldn't witness Yoda's fish if Yoda were to be eligible to win the tournament.

This particular tournament was a season-long one in which the most total inches won the prize. But one was supposed to always fish with the same partner. Ned Niawanda was Yoda's partner. Ned was out hunting on the last day of the tourney, and Yoda needed one more fish to win. He went out with Gomer and Goober on *Mr. 88.* They don't usually fish the middle of the day on weekends, because of boneheaded boat traffic, but it was October and nippy enough to keep most of the knuckleheads in port. The fleet from the Straits Musky Club was out, and several boats were trolling right around them.

Yoda became concerned that if seen with Gomer and Goober, he might forfeit his lead in the tournament. It became comical to watch him: whenever he went outside the cabin, he pulled a full face mask down over his head. He thought that Simon Anthony might recognize him and disqualify him from a victory that he felt was certainly in his grasp. It didn't occur to

Yoda that his big ears always stuck out, face mask or not. Simon Anthony is a guy who will watch you cheat, know you are doing it, and wait for you to make amends. That wait may be forever. The deception worked, and Yoda won. Nobody took that cheated-for victory to heart any more than Yoda, because "if you ain't cheatin', you ain't tryin'."

Yoda is not the only member of the Straits Musky Club who is a cheater. Almost all the old-timers have fished before the season opened. They've even videotaped their exploits and used photos for advertisements. It is a seasonal fishery on both sides of the Musky Straits, opening in late June. The DEC assumes that the big females are off the spawning beds and on the move to summer ranges by season's start. If a man fishes in late May or early June, he can find these breeders and catch them before they scatter.

A musky man who cheats justifies it by claiming that his expertise makes him unlikely to hurt the fish. Groovy Traynor went out one spring with Ike Borodino twice and with Bart Pilcher once, and they caught many monster fish. Slim Tomkins, musky guide, magazine field editor, and mythic local fisherman, was on Borodino's boat one of those times. They caught many fish on these exploits, released them all, and justified their crime by saying everyone used to do it. Groovy bragged about catching five fish averaging 30 pounds and one a little smaller. This proves both his lack of ethics and ignorance of mathematics.

Fishermen exaggerate their catches. Lying fishermen tend to believe their own stretchers long after others have discounted them. Having invested one's prestige in the tale, it would be self-defeating to admit that the prestige rests only on a pillar of braggadocio and bravado.

A prominent musky man uses an illegal gaff to land his fish. A gaff is legal in Canada but illegal to even possess in a boat on the US side of the straits. Such illegality is justified by stating that the gaff doesn't harm the fish. That is probably true. All laws can be broken. It's not likely one will get caught breaking game laws.

Chapter Five

ARE YOU HAVING A NICE EL NINO?

SAYINGS NUMBER 16 AND 17
Fish Hard but Smart/We Could be Out there Right Now

It was 1998, and *El Nino* had been changing the weather all around North America, including the straits. Instead of horrible weather, the straits area had weather of the mildest kind for northern climes. Two inches of snow were on record for February, while the normal was 20-something. For the first time in 15 years, the Upper Lake did not freeze, and the average winter temperature was the third-mildest since 1868. Whenever Bob Traynor and Goober would be in sight of the straits, Traynor would say, "We could be out there right now." Most of the time in this off-season he was right, and he would lapse into a reverie about what it would be like if he could fish muskies all year. Most people's reveries, religious or otherwise, are silent. Not Traynor's. He suffers from what Goober calls "brain vomit," where every thought that resides in his brain, no matter how repulsive, trivial, or scatological, must come flying out of his mouth. Goober's secret for withstanding this verbal effluvia is the same one many husbands use on their nagging wives: selective deafness. But even with many years of practice, Goober cannot always resist the temptation to set Traynor off on an orgy of self-justification.

"With the lack of ice this winter, you and Borodino and Tompkins and Pilcher are going to have to do your preseason poaching in March." Goober pointed this out knowing that Groovy would take the bait.

"It isn't poaching; it's preseason fishing. We never kept those fish. And I'm not going to do that anymore. Once was enough."

"Once with Bart, once with the garbage man, once with Tompkins. Does Johnny Lawrence pre-season fish? I can't remember all your lore."

"I never went with Tompkins. I'd forgotten I'd told you about Borodino."

"You must be losing it. You used to be able to keep your stretchers in order. Was Borodino a member of the sizable seven?" Goober was just warming up to hit him about the gaff.

"What's this sizable seven stuff? We just wanted our release director to quit keeping all the information to himself. We did it for the good of the club." Groovy could be astonishingly self righteous.

As mentioned earlier, the sizable seven is a political wing of the Straits Musky Club that ousted an original board member because he was too good a liar. The sizable seven's core group contained a fair number of preseason anglers who had convinced themselves that they weren't poaching when they took the huge females off the spawning beds for their own preseason pleasure.

Editor's Note: This practice of pre-season fishing is commonly known as poaching by game wardens.

Like many political splinter groups, the sizable seven broke up, after their coup, over the issue of using photographs of preseason fish in advertising and self-promotion. Traynor is interested in self-promotion but against advertising unless done by the guy who he's mooching off at present. Eventually, the sizable seven became Bart and the Wannabes.

"Face it, Bob, if you were offered preseason angling with the right guy, you'd jump all over it. Just like you poach stripers when it suits you and use the illegal gaff on your fish. You'll do anything that is good for Traynor."

"The gaff, the gaff is going to be legal for me this year," Traynor stammered. "I'm going to get a permit, and, besides, the gaff is better for the fish and doesn't hurt them at all. It's legal through the ice, so why shouldn't it be legal on the open water?"

"So, the standard should be whatever is good for Bob? Because Bob had fun tearing five 30-pound females off their nests before the season started, that's OK with Bob?" Goober spoke quietly, without looking up. He knew he was being heard.

"I told you, I'm never doing that again." Groovy replied. He had to justify himself. It isn't healthy to go around despising oneself. Of course, he does have his superiority as a fisherman to fall back on.

As Groovy got to know the members of the Straits Musky Club, he got better offers than going out with Gomer and Goober, and stiffing them became a habit. This tended to aggravate Gomer more than Goober. "Hey Gom, if you're going to be friends with Groovy, you're going to get ditched."

"I'm too old to get ditched." Gomer's wrath could be jump-started, too, with the right prodding.

Each time Groovy, now also called Stiffy, returned to fishing with Gomer and Goober, he acted more and more distant and made comments about "how you guys do it." Instead of gaining knowledge from those experts he knew, he would act confused. One time he wanted to try jigging, and Gomer and Goober went along until he couldn't find the buoys that he'd fished the previous night with Bart. He hadn't even been sneaking his Schnapps like he often did with Gomer and Goober. He wasn't much help in imparting what he learned by sucking up to the musky men, but he was fluent with criticism.

One time, when Goober and Groovy were talking he announced that Bart didn't think Gomer and Goober took the quest for Girthra seriously. They were accused of ignoring the tenet of Musky Bill to "fish hard but fish smart." This probably came from answering Bob's questions in a deliberately vague manner.

"How deep are we?" Groovy asked, letting out his line.

"Between 11 and 24 feet," replied Goober, who hadn't looked at the gauge.

Later on, Groovy asked, "How much line have you got out?" He no doubt wanted to clue them in to how Bart or Johnny or Slim would be doing it.

"Don't know, but it's the right amount." Gomer could be difficult, too.

Why would anyone expect a couple of guys named Gomer and Goober to do anything in a smart fashion?

Chapter Six

LET ME REITERATE

Be on the Right Spot at the Right Time;
Nothing Else Matters/If it Works, Do it Again

In the past several years, a theory of science called "chaos theory" has been developing. This is not chaos like a riot in Los Angeles but chaos meaning simple randomness and the interactions it causes.

Picture it this way: visualize a ramp like cub scouts use for their pinewood derby race. The ramp is very long and has many lanes. At the top of each lane is poised a marble. Behind these marbles stands God. First a few at a time, then randomly forever, God flicks one of the poised marbles to roll down its lane of the ramp.

Visualize further that at a point in this long ramp, the lanes disappear suddenly. Without lanes, the rolling marbles begin to bump into each other, causing them to veer wildly, and others to do the same. At this point along that ramp, it looks like that famous movie shot of dozens of mousetraps tripping after ping-pong balls are dropped on top of them.

Now, imagine those rolling marbles are things like the information needed to make a tree, animal, weather pattern, or other natural phenomenon. All the information needed to grow and reproduce, to iterate, is contained in that marble. So, all these

71

marbles are iterations of information, and their interactions are random because of all the different marbles on the track and the fact that they are bouncing into each other.

Finally, imagine that the time frame for the rolling marbles is millions of years. Some iterations are smothered by others and fail to go on. Others get so rare as to be believed gone, only to reappear when conditions change, like the cormorants on the Great Lakes. It is as if the marbles bounce off the track, or smack into others and get a harmonic boost, or get side-tracked or hung up along the way, only to be reactivated when hit by another marble. Iterations die out, some grow, and all change.

We see this kind of thing on a small scale in the lake. As lake pollution is decreased, the water begins to clear, the fish thrive, zebra mussels are introduced, the water clears more, the fish thrive more, the cormorants that were nearly wiped out by the pesticide DDT now reappear, and the cormorants thrive on the abundant fish. The lake now appears to be changing into a cold, clear, less-fertile lake from a warmer and weedier lake. Geology is not supposed to work that way, but what do we know? Lakes are supposed to change over time from clear, relatively infertile waters to weedier, siltier, more fertile waters.

Musky men would like to control all this so that fishing is excellent for them. Even more than their desire to control the ecology is their desire to believe they have the power to do so. Bob Traynor loves to get mad at the cormorants. They have roosted in a couple of trees on the Strand and Pirate Island. When they roost in a tree, they kill it with their guano, and it stands as a reminder of the changes wrought by the cormorants. The Straits Musky Club has worked to make these islands nature preserves, but Traynor wants permission to kill the cormorants.

There is another aspect of chaos theory, but it's even more difficult to describe. You've heard people use the expression "life's infinite variety." Well, actually, the variety is finite; it is the iterations that are infinite.

Trolling is the preferred fishing method in the straits, and it takes some time straining the water to catch muskies. During the long hours fishing, one notices the sounds out there. There is a rhythm from your engine that iterates: *vrmmm, mmm, mmm.* You also have the wind itself and the sounds it makes in the rigging: *woo-oo, woo-oo, woo-oo.* The waves lap against the boat's hull: *plish, swish.* The lines on the rods vibrate lightly *hmm.* The downrigger cable vibrates more strongly: *hrmm, hrmm, hrmm, ree, ree, ree.* The rods and the boat creak and snap with the shift of a heading. These repeated sounds hypnotize one into a religious state.

In October and November, there are few but the musky anglers about, and each one of them is trying to "be on the right spot at the right time; nothing else matters."

The season goes on with the sounds and the cold and the wind and the waves and the followers of Musky Bill trying to perfect the quest for Girthra. Sometimes the angler hits the right pattern and catches a musky, and then another, and perhaps even another by repeating the same run with the same lure. This can be luck, but the musky men prefer to believe that it is skill. They are savvy enough to know that "if it works, do it again."

A musky will fill a niche by occupying a good place to grab an easy meal. The most successful big female will have the best position. If she is removed, another musky will immediately occupy that niche. She will be the next biggest predator in the general area. If a prime spot is destroyed by natural or human causes—erosion or dredging, for example—she will move to the next closest prime spot. "If it works, do it again" is therefore the prime directive for both muskies and their pursuers.

Chapter Seven

WHAT ARE YOU DOING?

SAYING NUMBER 20

It's Great to Be (Not So) Smart

People around here have the Pantherville disease, which has thoroughly infected the board of directors of the Straits Musky Club. Pantherville disease afflicts one like this: one gets a job, joins a club, or begins an activity. Next, the activity pans out, in that one gets more involved and does more to include that in one's life. Then, the complaining starts: the activity is too much work, it takes up all of one's time, or why isn't someone else doing more? Constant complaining marks the chronic, end stages of the Pantherville disease.

The Straits Musky Club exists as a mutual admiration society. Most of the club's time is spent shining the medals the membership and the board present to each other. The board members vote themselves an exemption from dues, an exemption that they feel they deserve for all the work they put in clapping each other on the back and bragging about how well they are doing. They create awards and halls of fame for the purpose of handing these plaudits to each other. They become upset at any and all attempts by the general membership to retake the club from the anointed.

When an insurgent vice-presidential candidate was elected, the board took two actions: they ensconced the outgoing VP into a special at-large seat that was created without input from that rascally membership, and then they immediately went to work trying to unseat and denigrate the new VP. Just as FDR tried to pack the Supreme Court, the Straits Musky Club board packs its board with like-minded members.

Pantherville disease is widespread in Pantherville and all of its immediately surrounding areas. In fact, it infects people in all the Straits Settlements—Swampherst, the Southtowns, and almost any of the urban, suburban, and semi-rural areas around Pantherville that all describe themselves as being from Pantherville when they are talking to non-residents. Likewise, the fans of the local sports teams complain about a whole host of real or imagined wrongs they have suffered: wide right, no goal, no goal II, and illegal forward pass. People with the Pantherville disease are better off with the frustration of being losers; they wouldn't know how to behave as champions.

The city fathers complain all the time about the lack of jobs for their children, who have moved to North Carolina and elsewhere for work. Meanwhile, the only people starting any businesses around Pantherville are escapees from the socialist paradise of Canada (determined to become the Cuba of the North). Instead of a spirit of optimism and entrepreneurship, the people of Pantherville whine and pine for the old days when big steel or big auto would hire a guy, keep him for 25 years, and then hire his son, too, because he was a good worker. It isn't like that any more. It is especially not like that where big union and big government are all that's left clinging to an ideal past that never really existed.

Goober likes it that Pantherville is shrinking and, as a corollary, that the popularity of golf is skyrocketing. There is no traffic in Pantherville. As far as boating is concerned, the waters of the straits are uncrowded except for two or three summer weekends. Sure, Goober's kids will probably find jobs elsewhere, but that's the world today: they've got to make their way. Meanwhile, Goober appreciates the elbow room.

Sometimes, Goober catches fish in ways that aren't supposed to work. Goober studied the List of Forty and the admonition that "It's great to be smart." Goober likes to add the qualifier "not so" in front of the word "smart." If he didn't have ignorance going for him, he wouldn't try some of the dumb stuff that works.

One day, Goober and Gomer were on the Pantherville side of the straits, where a licensed fisherman may use two rods. In order to troll the extra rods, they put some casting lures behind the boat, 30 feet back and down 15 feet on downriggers. They pulled in two muskies that way even though neither Bart nor Slim Tomkins had ever heard of that pattern. They have also fished in places that are not supposed to have fish.

In fact, too dumb to know, they have successfully fished Eddie's Run, the narrows, the slot, various spots fishing suspended baits downstream, other spots high in the straits, and while concentrating on the CBGB run rather than the car wash. Goober remembers the day he was trout fishing below a dam and noticed a nimrod nearby who was fishing with a spinning rod upside down and reeled anti-clockwise. Goober politely asked if he was having any luck. The nimrod said "yes," and instead of holding up a few of the 8-inch hatchery trout that Goober expected, he showed off two about 2 feet long.

Goober and Gomer have fished the night spots in the daylight and the daylight spots in the night. They have fished downstream without bouncing bottom and bounced bottom where it wasn't supposed to be fruitful.

The board of the Straits Musky Club is blessed with several members who were touched by Ball—that is, they learned some of their musky knowledge or musky lore from Horace Ball, the all-time top straits musky hunter. It is well known in the straits that Horace Ball was the best student of Musky Bill and that being touched by Ball, trying out Marcus's runs, or having fished with Don Maynard or Eddie O'Chefski immediately confers status bordering on the heroic to any man who can make such a claim. Apparently, channeling the knowledge of Musky Bill while referring to Horace Ball is open to interpretation because when Johnny Lawrence instructs the membership in his very

successful techniques the other board members scoff and snort
and titter and act bored even though Johnny invokes the name
of Horace Ball and often draws a reverent gasp from the members. Johnny Lawrence has been touched by Ball but so have
members of the board.

Musky Bill does not reach us only through the living. A few
years ago, Goober and Gomer went to the musky prom as a father
and son team. While they were winning all the good stuff at the
raffle table, Goober sat next to Mrs. Bobby Darin, whose husband
was being honored at the prom. During the evening, Mrs. Darin
stated that before he died Bobby used to fish the East Strait during the day to good success. His favorite time was 3:00 PM.

One other thing to think about is who to fish with: a musky
man like Groovy Traynor, or the famous Chinese guest, Sum
Dum Gai. If one is fishing with Sum Dum Gai, one can use him
for his license and fish twice as many of the lures one wants. Sum
Dum Gai will appreciate the trip and be ecstatic with any musky
caught. A musky man like Groovy Traynor, on the other hand,
will insist on his own rod and reel and lures, which often cuts
one's chances in half. He will roll his eyes at all the inadequate
boat handling, poor driving, wrong lures, off speeds, and other
mistakes made by a musky boatman. Because he probably con-
tributes to the gas bill—while Sum Dum Gai does not—Traynor
can treat the captain like hired help by being free with his criticism and orders. Then sometimes you get cowardice from the
musky hunter that not even a teenage girl would show. Goober
once caught a small male musky, and after the successful release
attempted to slap hands with Aunt Flo. Aunt Flo pulled her hand
because she didn't want to get any musky slime on her.

Gomer never gets anything right, although he likes to think
he does some things semi-right. One night, he and Goober
caught three fish without employing any consistency and without following the dictates of Musky Bill. They caught one fish
going across current, one fish going up current, and the largest
one going downstream (horror of horrors, they were not even

bottom-bouncing on the downstream run). They caught one fish on lead core, one fish on spiderwire, and one fish on fireline. One fish was caught on white, one fish on black, and one fish on red Depth Raiders.

Another mistake that Gomer and Goober make is going counter to the stated advice of the heroic musky men who interpret the List of Forty Sayings of Musky Bill. One interpretation is that some areas are only night areas and are therefore to be avoided in daylight hours. Gomer and Goober, doing just the opposite, catch fish.

Another interpretation is that downstream fishing only works if you bounce the bottom. Goober and Gomer regularly fish downstream for suspended fish and catch fish up to 48 inches. Another interpretation is that bottom-crashing only works on the deeper parts of the East Strait and is a waste of time on the West Strait. Yet, Goober has landed a 50- inch monster while bottom-bouncing the Slot on the West Straits.

Let's face it, it is great to be not so smart.

PART THREE

MYTHIC TALES OF MUSKY LORE

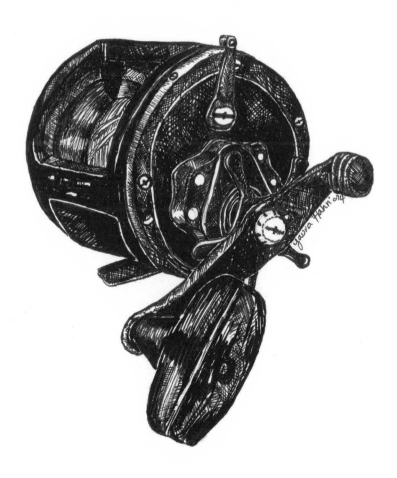

THE DREAM SEQUENCE

Finnegan Mincher had been dreaming so ferociously that he felt as if he hadn't slept for 7 days. He had been wandering around in a half-wakeful state for the past 3 days. These dreams had been compressing distance and time in a rapidly spinning world, and he had been to seven places in a dream world, although most were unfamiliar to him in actual experience. He moved rapidly from place to place, sometimes fishing, sometimes sitting at a table with fellow anglers, sometimes looking on from outside the places. Locations continually shuffled. The St. Larry, the Lake of the Woods, Cave Run Lake, The Ottawa River, The Musky Straits, The Chippewa Flowage, and Georgian Bay. A voice always intruded on this dream, saying something like this, in stentorian tones, "Here you will find the seven children of Girthra, the 12 grandchildren of Girthra, and the 40 great-grand-children of Girthra."

Finn met Commodore Gid for a walk at the canalway in Swampherst. Finn still had no idea how he knew when and where he was to meet Gid Gunmore; it just happened. Gid was of notable lineage. He had the Pantherville suburb of Gunmore named for his family and Butler Creek in Canada named for a maternal ancestor. He arrived inconspicuously in a Taurus, the notorious jellybean car. It was the plenilune, time of the full moon, and Finn's state of exhaustion filled him with a manic energy. He had a million questions for Commodore Gid.

"While *Epic Tales and Heroic Musky Hunters* is amusing and ironic, I don't get where this one page of Otto Conrad stuff is leading. What does it mean?"

"Otto is a moralist, so look to his suggestions as moral education. Musky fishing is an enterprise, not a hobby. Without a sense of morality and ceremony, you will end up a lush, like Ben Franks," Gid said. He then posed a question of Finn.

"Have you been dreaming lately?"

"Have I ever! It's been continuous."

"Tell me something about these dreams."

"They have been all over the place."

Gid nodded and gave Finn a knowing smile. Finn continued.

"Time and space don't seem to matter, but they all end up at a meeting of the Straits Musky Club."

"Go on," Gid said.

"I am at the detention table where the members in bad standing gather for meetings. Everyone is eyeing one another to judge relative status. The highest ranked are those who have been touched by Ball. He's the most famous of the legendary musky hunters from Tank's Livery."

"I'm well aware of Horace Ball," Gid said. Finn went on anyway as if he hadn't heard this. "Being 'touched by Ball' means having had experience in the old days, when every musky was killed and a man who had a 15-pound fish on the top-twenty board would still bring in a 12-pounder. It was through Horace Ball that the famous List of Forty, the sayings of Musky Bill, came to be known. Such people as Ike Borodino, Johnny Lawrence, Sheriff Andy, Simon Anthony, disgraced member Slim Tompkins, and disgraced and regraced member Magnus Markson are all touched by Ball. But are they mythic figures of musky lore? No! How can they be?"

Finn looked up to see how Gid was receiving this rhetorical question. Gid betrayed no emotion, and Finn continued.

"There is Magnus Markson, who wanted to be in a club where only he knew where to catch fish. When that didn't work out, he quit," Finn said. He paused before wading back in.

"How can the board members of the SMC be mythic when the half that aren't sharpening knives are the ones selling whetstones? They act like bureaucrats with a supercilious air brought on by a lifetime of caution, keeping the head down as the flak flies overhead, reveling in the raw power of denying everyone who doesn't follow their rules." Finn paused momentarily before continuing.

"Perhaps the late Dr. Mendele was a mythic figure. He never took himself too seriously. He could break balls with a laugh, a smile, a nod, or a wink. His watchword for living seemed to be gleaned from a package of firecrackers, 'Light fuse and retire smartly.'"

Finn went on, "Surely, Simon Anthony cannot be a mythic musky man, even though he is a very good fisherman and has the Tony factor in his favor. He took Dale Newfy along 31 times before Newfy even had a rod to fish. Then Newfy had to go another 54 times before he caught a musky. If Dale Newfy had gone with Goober and Gomer, he'd have landed 20 fish in that time." Finn paused one final time before concluding.

"Truly, the ones who have been touched by Ball have achieved heroic status. The Mythic ones are those who do not press so hard for their connection with Horace Ball and Musky Bill."

Finn heard a blues song on the wind with the line, "If you don't like my peaches/don't shake my tree."

Gid stated the obvious: "That sounds more like an essay than a dream."

"I know, but that part always fixes itself to my dream sequence. Then Musky Bo jumps up and says a bunch of unrelated things. Musky Bo is a columnist for the Straits Musky Club newsletter who writes anonymously and venomously in an effort to justify his superiority on all things related to muskies and musky fishing," Finn explained. He went on.

"He appears in my dream like the Roman God Janus. The two faces alternate between Simon Anthony and Tom Booker. He yells about preseason fishing. He skewers those who are too comfortable while fishing. He claims to have once caught many fish but to be impotent now. This diatribe is delivered in a monotone one moment and a lisp the next." Finn closed his eyes as he continued, as though struggling to see the image he is describing without being distracted. "Musky Bo then changes into King Lear facing down the tempest on a lonely headland, perhaps Dennehy's Wall. The spindrift whips around him as he works his rod over the weedbeds. Then, suddenly, Bo is behind the head table at the Straits Musky Club meeting, explaining how the government can solve all the issues of the club. At this point, the dream fades out, only to begin again after a visit to another of the seven rotating locations."

Finn sighed and opened his eyes, exhausted. Once more, he found himself alone with a sheet of sayings from Otto Conrad and a thin volume of musky tales from the sayings of Musky Bill.

THE QUEST FOR GIRTHRA

Zarathustra:
The tyrant madness of impotence cries for "equality;" thus, the most
secret tyrant appetite disguises itself in words of virtue. Equality is a
hidden vengefulness which seeks to destroy beauty and talent.

All fishermen talk like that; what they cannot fathom is unfathomable.

Statistics will always back up your argument
if you've already made up your mind.
Professor Smart

"Probe until you meet resistance;
there is where you will find the guilty conscience."
Sigmund Freud

It is common for an older man to oppose the indiscretions
of his youth with utmost vigor by assigning these faults to his
enemies. He is looking at his maker and trying desperately to undo
anything bad in God's big tally book. This is called transference and
is why so many old men turn in to hopeless cranks.

...And why too, when you have awaked and completely returned to
reality do you feel almost always, and sometimes with extraordinary
intensity, that you have left behind in your dreams a mystery you can-
not solve? You laugh at your dream's absurdities, and at the same time
you feel that in the fabric of those absurdities some thought is hidden...
Dostoevsky

4 ordeals...awake for 7 days...symbolic death...immortality
5 Valuable Goal...snake eats plant of eternal life...
separation of human and divine
Ishtar rebuffed by Gilgamesh

*"The process of creating a 'myth' to justify an action
need not be conscious."*
F.A. Hayek

Lack of reverence equals drift and ennui, a chronic sense of emptiness.

Read aloud the Revelation of Saint John from the New Testament.

Otto Conrad

Chapter One

THE ONLY EQUATION YOU NEED

Saying Number 21

$Ml=Mk+Mm$

Musky Lore Equals Musky Knowledge Plus Musky Myth

In November, when the days get very short and the darkness, without a moon, is a black plastic bag pulled over your eyes, Goober has trouble seeing and avoids going out as much as possible. Gomer was driving because he claims that his eyes are immune to aging and he's not bothered by all the health stuff that's bringing Goober down. They'd gotten their room and had their dinner and were getting the lay of the land around Clayton when they turned down an ordinary looking side street and found the town dock.

It sure looked small. There was one ramp about 12 feet wide with a series of nice wooden docks out into the river. As they parked their trailer with the 25-foot Wellcraft so that they could go look at the launch ramp, they came to the realization that because it was after dark in a strange place they'd be better off to launch in the morning. While scoping the area, they came upon Marcus Quimby, pulling his boat out after a day of fishing.

Marcus is tall and lanky without the layered clothing that Gomer and Goober wore to keep warm in the frosty November air. Though his coat seemed to have a little pile to it, one caught oneself shivering when looking at him the way one does when seeing idiotic bare-chested football fans at wintry games.

Marcus had greasy-looking gray curls of the Roman type that, after a day hatless on the St. Larry, looked as if they'd been combed with an egg-beater. His shoulders were slim and sloping and set off his round head to look almost like a caricature. The glasses he wore accentuated the large round character of his eye sockets and made him look owlish. He was perhaps in his late fifties or early sixties and a snowbird, sporting a Florida car and boat registration.

There are more of these snowbirds than one would think: the type who move to Florida and then miss the North. Everyone complains about the weather in upstate New York, but many men enjoy pursuits like hunting and spring, fall, and even winter fishing, all of which call for hardiness and a nonchalant attitude to the elements. These New Yorkers move to Florida at their wives' insistence and then come back several times per year for their sport of choice.

People who don't indulge in these sports find it hard to understand the attraction to them. Perhaps it's the cold-weather activity that necessitates an entire set of clothes and gear and toys with which one has no other chance to wear and play with except when hunting or fishing.

Marcus, however, was not one for gear. He was fishing in the St. Larry in early November and planning on fishing the Upper Strait in the two ensuing weeks. Perhaps it gets a little boring spending all one's time trying to figure out where to go for an early bird dinner in Florida. (While Gomer and Goober were away at the Larry, Marcus went to the straits and caught a 49-incher; he may hail from Florida but can't get enough of his New York muskies).

The St. Larry is *BIG* water. There is current and there is wind and there are ocean-going freighters that throw 4-foot wakes. Marcus was trailering his 14-foot aluminum boat. The boat's equipment consisted of four gas tanks, four rods and reels, a tackle box with a Polaroid camera in the top, and a small terrier dog.

Gomer offered to help Marcus get his boat on the trailer, but he was insistent on doing it himself. Unable to pull the boat up onto the trailer, he walked out on its tongue to get a rope off the bow of the boat. Walking the tongue of a trailer is a tricky maneuver, at best, even when one has something to steady one's balance against. In the middle of a boat slip, it is foolhardy.

One of the things that people who fish in late fall and winter pride themselves on is their hardiness. It is part of the mystique to be able to endure and conquer as well as to enjoy nature. Marcus was out on the big water at night wearing sweatpants, a light jacket, no hat, and a pair of Hush Puppies on his feet. These he proceeded to get pretty wet as he twice slipped off the tongue and had to dance back out of the water.

Eventually, Marcus got his boat out, and he talked about people he knew in the Straits Musky Club like Slim Tomkins and Ned Pugh. He told Gomer he'd heard of him by his business name, which wasn't likely. Underdressed, hatless, and poorly shod, Marcus had a self-effacing and stumbling manner that made one wonder whether he'd ever fished before. By contrast, one look at his boat made it obvious that he'd fished for years. His boat was well-equipped for man, dog, fuel, and gear. There was no place for a fishing partner in his boat.

After he'd pulled his rowboat, Marcus showed off his Polaroids, which he kept with the camera in the tackle box. All the photos had been taken on the water, with the islands of the St. Larry in the background. In all of them, Marcus's beady eyes and owlish glasses were enhanced by the Polaroid's harsh flash effect and the night scene to make Marcus's face look like two pie plates with tiny central holes and a grim, lipless mouth.

When they'd parted company with Marcus, Gomer and Goober concluded that the photos were so bad because Marcus had trained the dog to take them and the terrier wasn't very good with a flash. They did get a little more information from Marcus about the sayings of Musky Bill. Musky fishing is musky lore, and "musky lore equals musky knowledge plus musky myths."

Chapter Two

THE BUCKET BROTHERS
JOIN THE BHA

SAYING NUMBER 22

Real Fish Eat Lures

Gomer's preference for trolling over other styles of fishing is well known. Goober always thought the saying "real fish eat lures" came from his own experience. It wasn't until much later that he learned Musky Bill was responsible for that saying.

Musky lures are big and costly. As Groovy, Gomer, and Goober moved up the ladder of freshwater fish and got into musky fishing, Groovy bought hundreds of lures early on, and Gomer and Goober only had about two-dozen lures. At the time, Groovy was living on a trust fund and didn't work. He had no kids, no mortgage, and no car payment and could buy all the toys he wanted. Gomer and Goober had families and homes and kids to pay for and didn't apply the money to lures that Traynor did.

Some musky lures work and some don't. Sometimes none work.

One time, it was especially tough fishing. It was hot and sunny. The weather hadn't been changeable, which muskies prefer. It was mid-summer, and that meant weeds. The water was very clear. The rocketeers were out. The cigarette boats were out. The drunken, vulgar boatmen were out. It was crowded, and the boys weren't catching any muskies.

Goober was sitting at the lazy bench, waiting to reel in and clean one of the poles, when he found that Gomer had a little card with sticky eyeballs and prism tape in various colors. These stickers are used to decorate spoons and spinners for trout and salmon fishing. Goober took a couple of stick-on eyeballs and placed them on some lures in the place the vent would be on a real minnow. Gomer then got the idea of decorating lures and ran with it. Over the next few off-seasons, he decorated almost every lure he owned with prism tape, decals, model paints, and sloganeering. Each one thereby became a custom lure and started out with an eye for a butt hole, making it a member of the Butt Hole Army, or BHA. Undecorated lures were pledges until they could be customized and become full-fledged members of the BHA.

These custom crank-baits started their successful run one season with Bobby Darin's lure. Fishing lures come in many colors designed to catch fishermen and some colors designed to catch fish. Of these latter, two of the best are black and white. Bobby Darin started life as a white sucker Depth Raider. Though part of the rotation, he never had much success until Gomer slapped the third eye on him and cut some chartreuse prism tape for his sides. Goober thought the decorations reminded him of the fifties' flat-top hairdos and leaped from there to Bobby Darin. After being customized, Bobby went out and caught a fish within minutes. Bobby Darin caught the next six fish on *Mr. 88*. If one uses a lure often enough, something on the bottom will reach out and grab it. Eventually, Davy Jones got Bobby Darin. With Bobby Darin and his successors, the BHA was mustered.

Gomer's lure-customizing caused great hysterics at Bart's Tackle Plus, where the bums who hang around trying to out-lie each other laughed at the fools who'd ruined their lures. This was an example of the common trait among people to be dogmatic and inflexible about a subject of which they are somewhat knowledgeable. Traynor scoffs at the BHA and always fishes on Gomer's or Goober's boat with his own, better stuff. Bart once pointed out to Goober that there were no garish members of the

BHA in the musky book he was buying from him. Goober read the book. Custom lures were mentioned and recommended, but they didn't include any pictures. That explains why Bart had missed it.

Another source of amusement to Groovy Traynor were the buckets Gomer and Goober used to hold their lures. Musky lures are from 8 to 15 inches in length and don't fit into most tackle boxes used for other lures. They make special tackle boxes for musky lures, but these are huge and unwieldy. Gomer devised a method of hanging these long lures from the lip of a tall plastic pail, thereby keeping the hooks from snagging on anyone's clothes as people moved about within the boat.

Traynor, of course, has had three of the magnum boxes and has even given one away. Since Gomer and Goober had used buckets for a long time, Traynor made a point to tell his buddies at the Tackle Palace about how bush league Gomer and Goober were. They became known as the Bucket Brothers around the lazy bench at Bart's Minnows and Things. Traynor talks too much, and he made the mistake of using the term "Bucket Brothers" in conversation with Goober one time.

Shortly after *Booster* came into Goober's possession, he spent part of a Saturday setting up a new system for holding these big lures. He'd gotten two livewells with his boat, which were supposed to hold ice or water to store any fish going home to be eaten. These were no good as livewells because the engine heat made them quite warm and would melt any ice in them. Goober cut plastic pipe of the correct diameter and taped the pieces into modules which would fit in the livewell boxes and hold the lures upright yet be semi-portable. On the first day out with the new lure boxes, Gomer and Goober each got a legal fish (over 44 inches). That was the day when the Bucket Brothers became the Tube Twins.

Chapter Three

THREE KNOCKOFFS ARE ENOUGH

SAYING NUMBER 23

I Didn't Catch Any, but I Lost a 50-incher

Fishermen are justly famous for stories of the one that got away. Musky fishers, in pursuit of the legendary Girthra, tell legendary sagas of the one that got away, whether he was a short-hitter, threw the hook, or broke the line. Since some of the trips out musky fishing result in skunkage, or no fish, a missed fish can be an event. Some occasions of losing or missing a fish are spectacular, but the musky men go too far.

Goober was telling about Traynor and his holding forth with musky lore.

"After every time he'd been out with Bart, he'd be brimming to tell tales. If Bart had achieved a good catch and Bob could take credit for some of it, he'd be sure to tell us. Even if Bart didn't catch anything, he did it better than anyone else. Early on, he'd gone on about knockoffs and lost fish, but I'd bust his chops if he started talking about knockoffs. I even kidded Groovy that they kept a record of knockoffs at Bart's Bait Emporium."

In trolling the straits for muskies, one sets up with heavy rods, heavy line, and large reels, set on light drag with the clicker on. When a musky hits, the clicker screams as the line is pulled out. One jumps to the rod, strikes the fish by yanking back on the rod, and tightens the drag somewhat so the fish stops taking line. That clicker going off means "fish on" to a straits troller. The boat explodes into action when the reel screams.

Of course, catching weeds, the bottom, a sunken ship, or other structures will make that reel go off, too. In musky trolling, one often trolls in or near the weeds. Weeds are a common source of knockoffs. If one has the clicker explode but there is no fish on, the lure is brought in and checked for weeds. If no weeds are present, a knockoff is declared.

Many musky hunters have lost legitimate big fish while reeling in, as well as beside the boat. Muskies have a habit of following lures as they are reeled in, looking for a change in action to trigger a strike. They are certainly strong enough to break lines, leaders, lures, and hooks. They rip lures in half and pull hooks out of lures.

"Knockoffs happen to everyone, but only Bart's and Groovy's can be legendary. It got so bad, him making up lore about his times with Bart, that Gomer and I began to talk all the time about knockoffs. When he didn't stop with the trash talk, Gomer and I declared that each knockoff was now worth 12 inches toward a musky, and three knockoffs equaled a 3-foot musky," explained Goober.

Experience with smaller fish, where one can sometimes see the fish taking the lure, has shown that fish can inhale and reject a lure without the fisherman even noticing. They can mouth the lure but miss all the hooks on it.

"The thing with Traynor is he never just misses a fish: he misses a better fish than you, usually with better company, in a better boat. He's always missing a 50-incher. So one day he changed the topic to how much line he had pulled off his reel before his knockoff. Now we had to hear how his knockoff pulled out more line than any knockoff ever before. It doesn't take much for him to want to outdo you," Goober continued.

One of the lines which straits trollers use is called lead-core trolling line. This line is dyed a different color every 10 yards so that the fisherman can always tell how much line he has out. For example, when a straits troller says he's "out four colors," he's saying he's trolling 120 feet of line.

"So now when he wants to impress me about how much better his knockoffs are, he says, 'He ripped off a solid color before I could get to the rod, and he was gone.' That Groovy's quite a guy," Goober concluded.

At Bart's Fishing Tackle one day, Bart and Groovy were excoriating Tom Booker for his lack of speed in grabbing a rod when it went off. They had been fishing with Tom Booker the previous evening. It seems that Booker is a little harder of hearing (and older) than Pilcher or Traynor, and, though they call him their buddy, Bart and Groovy don't mind making fun of him for not being up to their standards as a musky man.

When you hear gossip coming to you, there will surely be gossip coming to others about you from the same person.

Chapter Four

A GUY WHO KNEW A GUY

SAYINGS NUMBER 24 AND 25

Remember What Flopp Did on the
Ottawa/Always Use the Hot Color

When one is out musky fishing in the Upper Straits, a good source for a small amount of information and a great deal of chatter is a certain channel on the VHF radio. One gets the feeling that there are far more listeners than talkers. It's sort of like the way old movies depicted a party line. As the hero spoke to his girl, a number of busybodies listened in. Even with most people listening, there still is some information broadcast on the VHF, and some of it is good.

The VHF is where Stock Boy first heard about Musky Bill. Stock Boy is a broker who likes to fish and wants to catch a big musky. One of his clients is a fellow with the radio name of Booster. He's an odd, duck, much older than Stock Boy, but he has a musky boat. He knows where at least some of the fish are located.

As Stock Boy went out with Booster one year to try catching a 'lunge from the straits, he began to hear rumors—sayings and lore about Musky Bill and his List of Forty. One of the fellows on the musky channel is the famous musky guide Slim Tomkins who runs charters under the handle of Big Hoggs. Though Booster is a quiet and self-effacing guy who doesn't tell him much about musky fishing because he claims to not know anything, he took Stock Boy out fishing four times that season and allowed him to pick up quite a bit of knowledge by observation.

One Saturday, they saw Slim Tomkins' boat as well as the boat of another famous musky man, Magnus Markson.

"You'll have to watch Markson's boat for tips. He knows a lot but won't talk on the radio since the sizable seven ran him out of the club. Tomkins will talk to you over the radio, although I seldom bother listening to it," declared Booster.

"What's his handle, and who are the sizable seven?" Stock Boy asked.

"He'll answer to Big Hogg or the name of his boat, which is *Sure Thing*," said Booster.

"Big Hogg, Big Hogg, this is Booster lookin'. Are your ears up?" Stock Boy said after keying the mike. "You've got to tell me about this sizable seven stuff," he said in an aside to Booster as he waited for Tomkins to respond.

"Who's out there looking for Big Hogg?"

"This is Booster. How you doing up there today? Are you at the head of the river?"

"Yeah, we're at the head of the river. No fish yet. Are you in that big boat following me?" asked Tomkins.

"Yep. Call us if you get anything. Booster on the side," he said, hanging up the mike.

Typically, the chatter on the VHF is as inconsequential as that. But it was on the radio that Stock Boy first heard the voice of Musky Bill. His wisdom penetrated the airwaves over the Upper Strait.

Two of the big users of the radio to compare catches, brag, or chitchat are Bart Pilcher and Johnny Lawrence. They either call out their catches or, in Bart's case, answer inquiries from the fleet of wannabes.

One of the things that this usage of the radio does is give everybody a nickname as his radio handle. Often this is the boat name, but it can just be a made up name. The people who choose their handles are subject to diminution, malapropism, and other nicknames derived from nicknames. This is how Stock Boy got his name on the musky channel.

That Saturday morning, as the early trollers were griping about their lack of success, Bart and his posse were talking about which color was the hot one. Since none of the fleet had any luck, this discussion seemed futile to Booster and Stock Boy as they listened aboard the *Booster*. Then, as the air went dead for a few seconds, an eerie, static-filled voice came across in a deep and resonant tone: "Remember what Flopp did on the Ottawa," it said. This command, which seemed to come from the scudding gray clouds rather than the tiny radio speaker, brought several moments of silence, then:

"What was that?"

"Did you hear that?"

"Tubby, Tubby, Tubby, what's happening?"

Tubby was Bart's radio handle.

More of these inquiries poured out of the radio as listeners stepped all over each other seeking reassurance from Bart.

"That was the voice of Musky Bill. I suggest you heed it." Bart had their attention now. He went on to explain that Musky Bill was always aware of those anglers visiting Bart's Bait Shop and telling wondrous tales of great fish. Floyd Koop, also known as Flopp, had recently returned from the Ottawa River, stating that a red lure flecked with silver sparkles had caught a fish over 50 inches and many smaller muskies.

"Then Traynor joined Gomer and Goober for one of their outings. He began talking about a lure pattern that he had used. He explained that it was a recommendation from Musky Bill, what Flopp had observed, how Bart backed up all the sayings of Musky Bill, and how Traynor had that lure and you didn't," Booster said.

The boys were skunked that night. Traynor never trolled the Flopp lure. Lure color does matter in several ways. Gomer and Goober run a rotation of lures in order to find a color that catches muskies in the particular conditions of the moment. The biggest variable is always the clarity of the water. In the Upper Straits, that can be anywhere from chocolate milk to transparent down to 18 feet. The sky, sun, moon, and many factors unknowable also affect the hot color. Hot colors do exist. When Gomer and Goober's rotation of lures hits a color that works, they will concentrate more on fishing the color that has been selected this way. Next time out, chances are good that conditions will have changed enough so that a different color will be hot.

Groovy uses a different theory. He has two or three "confidence baits," and he concentrates on running them all evening. Once, Goober was putting away the lures from their rotation when he grabbed an old disused lure, strode up to Gomer, who was motoring back to the dock, and said, "Here's the one O'Shaunnessy used at Leech Lake."

Gomer, being a good sport, said, "Did I have one of those?"

"Yep. That's the one from Leech Lake, the *hot* lure."

"Always use the hot color," said Gomer.

Chapter Five

EVEN AN OLD CAP'N GETS SEASICK

SAYING NUMBER 26

Never Eat a Crème-filled Cookie at Sea

Sometimes the sayings of Musky Bill have little or no relation to Bob Traynor or Bart Pilcher. Could it be that there are bogus sloganeers out there? The times when Gomer and Goober and Groovy went out on Gomer's boat went according to a pattern.

Everyone was responsible for his own lunch or snack and drinks. Some people brought something to share. There are only a limited number of items that Gomer will accept on *Mr. 88*. For example, beverages in cans or plastic bottles with screw caps are welcome; those in glass bottles are not. Chocolate is welcome— usually a Musky Bar (Three Musketeers)—but never any chocolate with nuts. Cookies can come aboard, but only those of the plainest type. Finally, pretzel rods, which are a staple of Gomer's diet, are always welcome. Goober would support Gomer on this last by droning on about the Roman army marching on a diet of pretzels. Goober related later, that on their trip to the St. Larry, Gomer displayed additional dietary quirks, including a daily dose of Frosted Flakes before he was able to function.

Usually Goober would bring some plain cookies, and Gomer supplied the pretzel rods. Just as Groovy didn't want to let a guest mechanic on Gomer's boat slide in front of him on the fish rotation, he usually didn't bring anything to share with "some mechanic I don't know." Goober tells of the time when Traynor showed up late, having gone to the local gourmet shop to buy some of their famous focaccio.

"This is the goods!" Groovy declared as he came aboard. During the ensuing 4 hours of fishing, Traynor proceeded to eat all this bread with gusto and accompanying it with great slurping noises and punctuating the gastronomy by sucking his teeth loudly and repeatedly. This was the typical Traynor behavior of showing you that what he had was better than what you had. Sometimes when Traynor brought some candy to share, he would seem to have a panic attack and grab back the candy and wedge it into his face as fast as he could.

The second time Stock Boy went out with these guys, he brought some cookies that had the dreaded crème filling. They were out in the Upper Lake that day, and the waves were crashing over the breakwalls at the head of the straits. These waves were the big 6- and 7-foot rollers with a wavelength of 30 or 40 feet. Because it seems as if they come all the way down the lake while building in intensity, they are different from the choppy, short whitecaps that often roil up on a localized blow.

The big rollers are quite intense in a bigger boat and nearly impossible to weather in a small boat. These swells tower above the transom of the boat by several feet as they follow the craft. A man looking back at the trolling lines has the experience of looking up at a wall of water chasing him and which seems ready to overwhelm the boat but actually just pushes it along. As long as the captain trolls with the waves, these rollers don't pitch one about in the cockpit of the boat but they do give one's knees a workout shifting weight back and forth.

Gomer wasn't seated much this night as he worked the back deck to keep the shifting of the weight in the boat to a minimum. He isn't as heavy as Goober or Groovy and is quite nimble in the boat. When he moves around, he is able to maintain his balance quite well. That workout turned Gomer's stomach upside down, and by the time they were heading back to the calmer waters of the Strait, he was draped over the engine box moaning the words of Musky Bill, "Never eat a crème-filled cookie at sea." Goober snapped a photo of the captain in distress and later had it framed as a reminder of the sayings of Musky Bill and their efficacy in the quest for Girthra.

Chapter Six

DO YOU WANT OLDIES
OR GOAT ROPERS?

SAYING NUMBER 27
There's No Such Thing as Musky Music

We've shown previously that the sounds of musky fishing are a large part of the total experience. These are the sounds caused by wind and wave and rigging and tackle. What else does a musky hunter hear out there? There is conversation in the boat among the anglers. There is chatter over the VHF radio. There are sounds from shore and passing boats.

And there is music from the commercial radio or tape player.

One of the reasons musky fishing is more of a guy thing than a gal thing is the lack of conversation.

"How can you sit in a boat for all that time and not talk?" was the first question Goober's wife asked when he started taking up the sport. At that time, Goober had a management job wherein all he did all day was talk to people, so he replied, "That's the good part about it for me."

Musky fishermen are not bound by any sort of vow of silence. They talk about the mechanics of the work they are engaged in. Excessive prattle about nothing and repetition are looked down upon by musky men. While Aunt Flo can't seem to stop herself from constantly running on about all the people she knows and how much they like her, Groovy Traynor either brags in an obnoxious manner or goes into a pout from which he doesn't even acknowledge one's existence. These are both examples of unwelcome conversation.

The VHF radio is another source of unnatural sound on the water, and one has to blame Bart Pilcher for a large amount of that. His status as a worm broker makes Bart not only a personable guy but one who knows a large number of anglers as well as wannabes. When it wasn't hunting season, Bart used to spend a lot of evenings fishing the Upper Straits, and even when he wasn't out there his posse was looking for him. This group was always on the radio asking Bart where he was and what he would advise about some situation like floating weeds in the East Upper Straits. Occasionally Bart's wife Jessica gets on the radio and talks to members of the posse. She has a tendency to go beyond prudence and affect Bart's reputation by saying too much.

"Bart hasn't had a fish in the last six trips," she said over the air one night when Goober was out with a petulant Traynor. Another guy who likes the radio quite a bit is Hal Goulash, who tends to emit general broadcasts to any member of the Straits Musky Club. Gomer and Goober are occasional users of the airwaves, but it tends to go against their stealth maneuvers. The VHF has the advantage of an on/off switch.

Noises from the shorelines, air traffic, and other boats cannot be switched off and generally must be endured. The New York side of the Upper Straits is metropolitan, and the city fathers laid an interstate highway along the shore. Therefore, that side of the Strait offers the roar of traffic, the sounds of construction, the blare of sirens, and other civilized noises. The Canadian side is much more bucolic. Though it has a river road, it is much quieter and the preferred side to fish for this reason as well as others. Goober has expressed a wish for Canada to make more noise because it has shown a habit of sneaking up on him and trying to crash into his boat.

The noise made by boaters is generally not bad because they try to keep their distance from other boats. The exception to this is the cancer men in their cigarette boats. These boats are all engine, incredibly fast, and unbelievably loud. Some are American and some are Canadian advertising bad Canadian cigarettes. These boats roar up and down the straits, burning hundreds of dollars in gas as they compensate for the unendowed status that heredity and nature have visited upon the boaters.

Air traffic isn't a big noise problem because the jet airliners tend to head out over the lake and are at high altitude. There is a certain romantic aspect to some air traffic, as well. Gomer and Goober and Groovy were out on one of their Wednesday night excursions when a World War II vintage fighter plane flew over them, dipping its wingtips at them. This may have been Commodore Gid channeling. He was probably getting ready for the air show at the Cascades Air National Guard base to take place a few days later. The guard base also sends off two submarine hunters each Wednesday for training, and Gomer and Goober look forward to seeing them head out over the Upper Lake.

The FM radio is a different story because here one can choose one's noise. The choices of musky men usually come down to the following: country, for the gunrack redneck set; oldies, for the long-in-the-tooth aging baby-boomers; or alternative rock, for the gen-Xers. Problems are associated with each of these choices, which can be explained by examining how Gomer and Goober handle the music on their boats.

The most important sound on a musky boat is the scream of the reel as Girthra rips out line. *Nothing should be allowed to interfere with that sound.* This is why Musky Bill says, "there is no such thing as musky music. "

But a musky man also spends many hours trolling the straits and needs some diversion for his mind. Rock music needs to be loud to be appreciated. By interfering with the reel's scream, it is thereby the least desirable musky music. Country music has a high stupidity quotient, which makes it only a limited alternative. Oldies suffer from two problems: The Herman's Hermits come up too often, and the words to most songs are familiar to

Traynor, so that he feels inclined to either sing along or invent new words while singing along. Goober went so far as to offer Groovy a quarter for every song he didn't sing along with. Groovy couldn't earn 50 cents that way.

Gomer likes to listen to alternative rock, partly to show how young at heart and with-it he is but also, others suspect, because Groovy doesn't have any idea of the words and therefore can't sing along. To that end, Gomer listens to offbeat stations that sometimes go off the air, like the Planet, and his latest, the River. He also brings tapes, which he believes are cooler than all get out, and subjects his fishing partners to his tastes. Groovy also has a tendency to think his homemade tapes are God's gift to the listening public.

Occasionally, Otis comes along to drive the boat. When he is the driver, Otis scales back on his drinking and only has one Bacardi and Coke. That one drink is the size of a small oil drum. Otis likes to try inducing the muskies to bite by switching the stations at the right time. Since he is, like Hank Williams, Jr., a cross between rock and country, he tends to switch between these two. One time, when he switched from the goat-ropin' country music to the Planet (now, the River), a big musky hit Timmy Sledge's lure at that exact instant, and Otis took credit for the strike.

Goober's tastes tend to be wacky. He likes folk music, which his kids call whiny protest music. He listens to the blues, which he finds appropriate to the lot of the musky angler, who often comes back flying the Pepe LePew flag. The blues are too black for some musky men. Goober likes classical music, especially when he is trying to dock his boat in the marina, as he feels his mind gets more focused that way. If you have ever seen Goober dock his boat, you would understand his need for focus. Gomer noticed a classical tape on the boat one day and asked if it had been thrown in with the purchase of the boat. Last season, Goober started listening to broadcasts of baseball games. They take a long time and give the musky fishing a sense of continuity. Baseball season ends prior to musky season, however.

Sometimes silence is the best musky music, and even Gomer asks for the radio to be off. Musky Bill is right again. The digital age has brought an additional plague to the musky hunter, and that is the cellular phone. Groovy Traynor has a new-fangled cellular phone with a walkie-talkie feature that enables him to speak with his brother Donnie at the press of one button. Not only does Traynor stand in the back corner of the boat and talk into this thing about the most mundane and trivial matters, he talks about Goober in a snide and deprecating manner while he is on Goober's boat. Never let it be said that no bad things can happen from a mother telling her boy he is cute.

Chapter Seven

THAT'LL BE CLIPPING ON FLO

SAYING NUMBER 28
Punt Coverage Rules Apply on Deck

Because the Upper Lake and the Lower Lake are Big Waters that have created the straits between them, a musky fisherman needs a good-sized boat with at least a semi-vee bottom. Flat bottom boats cannot stand up to the big rollers and breakers of these waters with safety.

A larger boat takes a pounding better and takes less water over the bow. No one but Johnny Lawrence goes out in the really heavy seas. In November, the Pantherville Harbor can get huge waves from high winds lasting for days; this is the Alberta Clipper warming up for winter. The waves can break over the top of Poot's lakeside restaurant, which is a two-story building that is built 10 feet above normal water level.

A larger boat can create its own set of problems. *Mr. 88* and *Booster* each have a cabin, a cockpit, and a bridge. This design allows crew and guests the luxury of walking around some while tending the fishing rods or just enjoying life. The cockpit is the rear deck of the boat where the motor cover is located and the actual setting out and reeling in of the lures occurs. It is also where the action takes place when a rod goes off. It is a well-known fact of musky fishing that the fish will not bite unless the angler is otherwise occupied—for example, eating a sandwich, emptying his bladder, tying a leader, or searching for something.

As mentioned previously, the trolling technique is to put out the rods with a light setting on the drag and the clicker in the "on" position. The striking fish then creates a rapid, loud clicking sound from the reel. Upon hearing this buzz, the fisherman sprints to the rod and, while grabbing it, places his thumb on the spool to arrest the removal of line. Then he immediately strikes against the fish to set the hook. The drag is then tightened most of the way down, leaving it just loose enough that a hard-fighting fish can pull out line without breaking it or the rod.

Getting to that screaming rod first is the climactic moment in musky fishing.

Gomer and Goober both fish the previously described rotation method, wherein a person is "up" on all rods being fished until he catches one. Then, the next person in the rotation is up. The exception to the rotation is a "right of discovery" fish. This is a fish that is caught as an angler is letting out or reeling in the line. Otherwise, if one is nearest to the rod that goes off, one grabs it, sets the hook, and hands it off to the person who is up.

When all the anglers are on the bridge seeking warmth, dryness, camaraderie, or refreshments, the strike scream of a musky rod going off will entail a mad dash for the rod. The pilot usually perks up his attention to the controls while all the other fishermen pay attention to the rod. If an angler doesn't grab that rod and hook the fish quickly, the fish may not get hooked and be lost. It is at this climactic moment that Musky Bill's admonition, "punt coverage rules apply on deck," obtains.

As any football fan knows, the punt is an especially dangerous play. With all players running at full speed, hits from many angles can be deadly to knees and ankles. The same is true for the cockpit of a musky boat with Gomer, Goober, and Aunt Flo all diving for the same corner. Blocking from behind, both above or below the waist, and any block below the waist are illegal. Players cannot be ridden out of bounds (i.e., overboard). The player fielding the musky rod must be given a one-yard cushion to complete the catch. A player in control may raise his hand and wave to indicate a fair catch. A muffed musky rod may be recovered by any player. Interference with a fair catch is illegal and punishable by being left on the nearest available dry land.

Musky Bill had the vision to see that without these rules, musky fishing would be an injury-riddled sport.

However, within the restrictions of these rules, the rush for the musky rod is still like the overtime period in hockey, where the "no call" is the predominant form of officiating. The biggest dog-whips and elbowing and kneeing from behind are commonplace—and largely overlooked.

The chaos that formerly existed on *Mr. 88* is an example of what can happen to those who fail to heed Musky Bill.

Gomer is a smaller and wirier guy than Aunt Flo or Goober, and, although all are geezers, Gomer is fairly agile. Flo is sizable in the extreme and as deft as a hippo on skates. Goober falls between the two in size, considerably larger than Gomer but less clunky than Aunt Flo.

Formerly. when a rod went off on *Mr. 88*, anyone or everyone might charge for it in order to strike at the fish. Gomer would dash around Aunt Flo to sneak ahead. Goober would get bowled over by Flo and sent flying. The laws of inertia favored Gomer, in that he can get underway easier, but once Flo's bulk is in motion, it is unstoppable. The arthritic Goober, a fair high school footballer, once knocked Gomer into the engine cover, causing a knee sprain. After this accident, Gomer and Goober and Flo were happy to re-read the words of Musky Bill and actually have them spoken aloud. The training involved in studying the List of Forty is vital in the search for Girthra, and nowhere is this more self-evident than in ensuring that everyone aboard understands Musky Bill's dictum that "punt coverage rules apply on deck."

PART FOUR

THE TONY FACTOR

THE DREAM TIME

It had become clear to Finn Mincher—through his encounters with Gid Gunmore; the quotes and items attributed to Otto Conrad; the increasingly intense, almost hallucinatory, dreaming; and the sayings of Musky Bill—that Gunmore was a superior man who represented the manly virtues of strength, wisdom, honor, and duty. Finn didn't have a handle on Otto Conrad yet but planned to ask Gid at their next meeting.

Gid showed up at one end of the riverwalk in Tiniwina, one of the towns of the Straits Stretches, in a Land Rover with the word "Wilderness" stenciled on its side. Finn strolled up to the driver's side window.

"We'll leave your truck here and ride up to the other end in mine," said Gid. Finn walked around to the passenger's side door and saw that the decal on this side of the vehicle read "Wildness."

"Let's re-spot the flight deck here," Gunmore said as he moved aside some items from the passenger seat and set them in the back. It seemed to Finn that he had hardly sat down and closed the door, when the vehicle was 3 miles up the riverwalk and Gunmore was getting out. This seemingly instant travel and the other dreamlike aspects of dealing with Admiral Gid no longer surprised Finn.

These meetings with Gid had made Finn do what he always did when a subject piqued his interest: read. He went to the library and read the limited items there. He went on the Internet and looked for resources, but all the while being careful about the crazy stuff so abundant there. He went to bookstores and bought books. And he began to learn about dreaming and Jung and dream work.

Finn used Robert A. Johnson's inner work method to stitch those dreams together. Johnson says that by working upon awakening to recreate the matrix of a dream, one could construct those connections in time and space that are so disjointed in retrospect. Johnson saw how the elements of dreams that are human nature (the collective unconscious) combine with the elements that are unique to the dreamer to create tableaux that cannot necessarily resolve conflicts but can explain them.

Finn had vividly remembered his father's gradual decent into dementia, when all manner of unresolved dissonance, issues, and just random thoughts would take possession of his father in the middle of the night. He had brought up a moral conflict from 30 years before. His brother-in-law had been stealing pies from the bakery he worked for and selling them on his own account. Apparently, he had hidden those stolen pies in Finn's father's vehicle one time, and Finn's Dad had carried a guilty conscience about those pies ever since. Another night, Finn's Dad had awakened and wandered off to tell a man that he would not be scoutmaster for another term. The police found him two streets over, in pajamas and fedora, looking for a house number from 35 years before.

It was the way that the dementia manifested long-repressed friction that made Finn think of his musky dreams. Was this how it worked? If he was able to work with his dreams, could he somehow link those unconnected thoughts into something he could work with? Was this what they were talking about with this channeling crap? All kinds of his Dad's sayings were catalogued in his mind, and they came up at many an odd time for comment or thought. When the connection was not obvious, could the dream work make sense of it?

Finn knew how the unresolved issues he wanted to discuss with his father created haunts in his mind that would bedevil him. He had his repressed issues, too. He'd hit a car and driven away, telling no one. He'd said the mean thing many a time, just to prove he had some kind of warped courage. He had a self-destructive gene that made him wreck good things. He sometimes lived his life as if for an audience—that audience being the man he wished he were.

Fishing was communication to an alien world through a string. Maybe dreaming was communication with the past in a similar way.

Finn left the Land Rover and glanced at the side, where the decal now read "Weirdness."

Gunmore began to walk south, and Mincher went around the car to catch up. He noticed that the decal on the driver's side now read "Wildman." Finn hurried on, torn between anticipation and dread, trying to catch up with Gid. He soon fell into stride with his mentor.

The next part of the musky lore is the most difficult part," Gunmore started explaining as he walked. Finn looked back at the white Land Rover where the decal now read "Willingness."

"To understand the Tony Factor, one must surrender oneself to the collective unconscious. All those pages from Otto Conrad and references to Freud and Jung and ritual and ceremony now come into play as you suspend disbelief in order to comprehend the effect of the Tony Factor, or lack thereof, upon your life."

"The Tony Factor? What the hell is the Tony Factor?" Finn asked. "Is this why my dreams are becoming so intense?"

"Dreams are messages from God delivered through the collective unconscious. When you first came to me, you were asking for directions—but in a symbolic way. Our meetings have been my method of moving you and your psyche in the direction of where they need to go for your next battle. You will see very little of me in the future," Gid said.

"But, I have to ask you about Otto Conrad and what he means!"

"You will know soon that he is the embodiment of moral virtue." Finn looked down and saw that he had his usual handouts, a few sheets from Otto Conrad and the usual thin volume, and now Gid Gunmore was gone. He'd walked 3 miles, he guessed, because there was his truck and he'd come to the end of the Riverwalk.

Mincher stepped over to a bench. He watched the water of the straits roll by and felt exhausted, as if he'd fought a great wrestling match with an opponent exactly as strong as himself. He also felt as if a weight had been taken from his shoulders. After a few minutes of watching the water flow, he went to his car and drove away.

Lord Nelson said, "You must expect your subordinates to tack against
the wind occasionally."

"Already a legend was growing up about me . It was suggested that I
used unconventional methods and there is nothing a professional
group mistrusts so nervously as it does anything that appears unconventional, and that has not been thoroughly written up in the jour-
nals. It may be quackery. Worse still, it may be effective. And if it is
both quackery and effective, it is utterly hateful."
"The Cunning Man "
Robertson Davies

Ritual is a means of approaching the inner world that the human race
evolved earlier in its history.... a highly ritualized symbolic act to
approach the inner world... ceremony = awe.
Ceremony became a way of behaving when one felt a sense of awe or
stood in awe.
The formality of religious ceremony indicates reverence and awe.
Ritual came spontaneously into being among all the peoples
of the earth.
C. Jung

"The minority, who will retain an inclination to criticize,
must all be silenced."
F. A. Hayek

Number Magic20 House
20 Corner
20th Fish
Twin 20s

Tony the Tiger, Shamblin' Tony, Ticklin' Tony, Antwan, Antoinette,
Antonin, Tanya, Honorary Tonys, Honorable Tonys, The Reel Man,

Dream time...Message from the Gods...collective unconscious
6. Homecoming

Once one gets hooked on the state, it's a rare man
who fights his way back to liberty.

Otto Conrad

Introduction

THE SURPRISING ANSWER

SAYING NUMBER 29

Get to Know Plenty of Tonys, and You'll Have a Happy Life

Familiarity with the sayings of Musky Bill will remind one of the elevation of Ticklin' Tony to the status of number one. While he is Tony Number One when he's tickling your engine, the sobriquet Tony Number One is fluid in nature.

Let us explain about Pantherville and the rest of the Straits Settlements. This is ethnic country, and each ethnic group drops the name Tony on lots of folks, boys and girls. We've got Polish Tonys, Irish Tonys, Puerto Rican Tonys, Black Tonys, and every Italian family has at least one Tony.

All of these ethnic groups and more have been mixing for years, but they always find safe water in naming a kid Tony or one of its variants: Antoine (sometimes spelled imaginatively or phonetically), Tanya, Antonia, or Antoinette. Anthony can be a first, middle, or last name, or even a nickname, and still qualify for the magic known as the "Tony Factor."

Only when Goober got sufficient Tonys working for him did he reach the level of becoming a happy man. That's when he began to notice the Tony Factor. He's got a mechanic named Tony, an outdrive expert named Tony, a lawyer named Tony, and the shadow president of the Straits Musky Club is a Tony.

So, are four Tonys the right number for contentment? Maybe, but let's look a little deeper.

One could have a barber named Tony (although that Tony was unable to deliver the Stanley Cup). Tony the Tiger could be on your side with a bowl each morning, as he is for Gomer. Surely, one has Tonys for neighbors, uncles, or siblings.

Does a person named Tony automatically have a happy life? Unfortunately for them, Tonys are not automatically benefited by the Tony Factor because, while having Tonys in your life improves your chances for felicity, it is not a sure thing. This positive effect of the Tony Factor means that even the Tonys need Tonys.

In Pantherville, they elect Tonys as mayors. Once, they elected a Stanley, and they suffered 4 years of blizzards as punishment. When they had a Jimmy as mayor for four terms, they stagnated—although he must have had Tonys in his administration to prevent backsliding. The city tried to undergo a rebirth under the administration of a guy named Tony. He must not have hired enough Tonys, as he has fallen on hard times.

There was a reel repair expert in the Straits Settlements named Tony. Several people went into business to try cutting into his monopoly, but most residents of the Straits Settlements wouldn't risk moving away from this Tony. The competitors of Tony invariably fail because the collective unconscious, hard wired into the human brain, steers people to the most readily available Tony.

Goober worked in a factory without any Tonys, and it was constantly in trouble. Without any Tonys, there was continual strife, quality problems, and poor profits. In areas where the ethnic mix doesn't provide enough Tonys, times are hard. It is a known fact that the happy people are the ones with Tonys working for them.

Understanding the Tony Factor takes some maturity. One must have the Tonys working for him. They have no value just lying around. They must be mechanics, contractors, barbers, lawyers, doctors, accountants, or others directly involved in one's life. Tonys have no capacity for evil. They are no good at whammies (it should be noted here that JohnJohn is handy with a whammy once in a while), curses, or hexes. Tonys cannot necessarily even help and can't give themselves a boost, but they can do no harm. If things in your life aren't good with the number of Tonys you've got working for you, simply get more Tonys.

As far as musky fishing is concerned, the Tony Factor combines the ceremonial, mythic, heroic, magical, and epic aspects to bring luck and satisfaction to the man wise enough to get plenty of Tonys and have a happy life.

Chapter One

A ONE, AND A TWO, AND A THREE, AND A FOUR

SAYINGS NUMBER 30 AND 31

Ticklin' Tony is the Only Tony/I Could Catch One Right Here

Gomer's business takes him into the land of the mechanics. Around the straits, that is a land with many Tonys. Gomer can't remember much, so instead of Tonys having last names, they've got numbers and nicknames. In Gomer's tales, he'll talk about "Tony One" and "Tony Four," and so forth. It's pretty confusing for the listener, but it does take away the burden of comprehending.

The really important guy, however, is Tony Number One, also known as Ticklin' Tony, or Tony Loud. Ticklin' Tony is a superior mechanic who got his name from his ability to "tickle" the engine into submission until it hits the state of perfect running. This ability has been witnessed and documented.

Another characteristic of these mechanics is that they usually have a finger or two that has been rounded off. Sometimes they are rounded down quite short. It's this rounded finger that goes in under the carb to tickle the engine into cool running. Tony Loud also promotes a special metal treatment compound, which he calls "schmozl," that helps in the performance of engine magic. Tony Number One has a life, however, and is not always available when repairs are needed. In such instances when that happens, Tony Two comes into the picture. Tony Two is also called Shamblin' Tony.

After Goober got his new old boat late in the season, Tony Two was enlisted for some repairs. Gomer and Goober already had plans for the St. Larry in November, so the boat's engine and stern drive had to be checked out. Tony found some problems that appeared to be the boat dealer's Band-Aid attempts to get the boat running well enough to sell. The propeller was also partially spun, which meant it could fail catastrophically. The stern drive needed some lubrication.

All of these repairs were supposedly effected at Tony Two's shop, and Goober and Gomer trailered the boat to the marina. The minute they started the engine, Gomer knew things were worse and the boat had to go back. Goober argued that Tony Two owed them a correct tune-up. The boat sat in a slip in the marina while the problem of only one bank of its V-8 firing was worked out. It took several trials and tribulations and three visits from Ticklin' Tony (Tony One) to get it right.

This is the story of the second to the last visit of Ticklin' Tony.

One thing about mechanics is that they have pride in being known as a good wrench. However, deep insecurity lurks just beneath the surface of their pride. When it gets down to specific cases, there are two people who mechanics have to outperform: any non-mechanic around, such as a "suit," and the last guy to work on the engine, who invariably has made the job more difficult. Tony One was now scheduled to fix the *Booster*.

Tony One showed up, with his 81 toolboxes, and began to methodically replace a number of components. Groovy and Goober helped carry the equipment needed down to the slip. It was found that new plugs and wires would be required. Goober went off for some spark plugs and wires.

"You see those initials on the engine, GM?" Tony One asked. "That's an American engine. So get me American plugs—Autolite, Champion, AC—just no Jap stuff," he said and showed Goober the Nissan plug he held in his hand with disgust.

Even though Goober drives a boat, its engine is a Chevy car engine, and it is an old one, from 1981. He started after the parts thinking about poor Tony One, down in the cockpit of that boat with Groovy up on the finger pier, running off at the mouth and casting giant lures above his head.

As Tony worked and Goober helpered, Bob was up there cheering them on. He'd brought his rain gear, four rods, and a tackle box half the size of a steamer trunk. He had two of these rods hooked up with 10-inch musky plugs. Every few minutes he'd say, "I could catch one right here." Then you'd hear him exhale in a swoosh and grunt as a *clackety-clackety* sound would whiz past.

It was the size and sound of a Lionel locomotive, and it was just a few inches above Tony's head. It was late in the boating season, and most of the slips in the marina were empty, giving Groovy plenty of room to cast. All the while, Traynor talked about how great the musky fishing would be in June, on opening day, next season. In June, he will talk about how good it's going to be in November.

Goober drove to the nearest car parts store on Straits Street. The guy at the counter explained, "We don't got no boat parts and wouldn't know how to look them up."

Goober went across the street to the marine store. They have a nice clean store, and the staff is friendly and helpful, but they don't know anything. Goober went to the sparkplug area and tried to match his engine with the appropriate plug. The only cross-reference chart there was for the dreaded Japanese plugs that Tony had warned against. But Goober was able to do a bass-ackwards cross-reference to end up with Champion plugs. He tried to do the same with wires, and back to the boat he went.

Tony grabbed the new plugs from him, rolled his eyes, and held the two together while extolling the virtues of the heavy iron Yankee equipment. Goober, being Goober, had completely nutsed up the wires and was sent off to NAPA to get the right stuff. As he hunted for the nearest NAPA, he thought about what

Gomer had said the night before, "Now you gotta keep Groovy away from Tony. He doesn't want to hear that Grandfather's Island smack."

"You mean the grandfather, wrong-island story?"

"That's the one."

"I'll do my best."

He'd said that, and here Goober was driving around visiting with motorheads while Groovy piled it on Tony. These Tonys come in all types. Tony Two is a big sleepy guy who doesn't seem like he is even moving. Tony Four, a mechanic turned barber, is an excitable talker who can out-yip Traynor. Tony One is a genuinely nice guy and is too polite to put a stop to Groovy like Tony Five had done one night by asking him, "Who cares about your grandfather?"

Eventually, Goober got back with plug wires, which he uncoiled and laid out and Tony installed. As it approached the hour when Tony had to get to work, they were double humpin' to get done and the toy locomotives clattered around their ears as Groovy fished and quoted Musky Bill again and again. When it became obvious that Tony had got it at least nearly right, Goober said, "Tony, you're the man!"

At that point, another quotation of Musky Bill came out of Traynor's mouth: "Ticklin' Tony is the only Tony."

Chapter Two

BART AND I NEVER GET TANGLED

SAYING NUMBER 32
Tune Your Lures

Goober sometimes does everything wrong. When he is having a good day, he does *almost* everything wrong. Stock Boy is his broker and shouldn't speak ill of his clients, but the truths from Musky Bill are of surpassing importance on the quest for Girthra. Stock Boy was along on the *Booster* one time when Goober proved his nickname was apt.

They were trolling three rods with four people in the boat. When running flat lines, or those not attached to downriggers, it is unusual to run more than three if one wishes to avoid tangles. Tangles can be a monster problem, especially after dark, with three big treble hooks on each lure and leaders that get kinked and swivels and snaps thrown into the inevitable bird's nest. Often, everything has to be cut off and new terminal tackle constructed.

Three flat lines can tangle if the driver makes too energetic a turn. They can also tangle if the center lure has too much movement from side to side. They can likewise get snarled if one of the outside lures runs out of line to the inside. A good pattern is to try using a deeper diver in the center and on a shorter lead. Musky Bill's advice to always "tune your lures" is vital to a successful pattern.

Lures just out of the package can run straight, but they often run out to either the left or right. Some lures run out so badly that they turn right over and pop to the surface, upside down. Usually, the hook eye in the front of the lure or the diving lip on lures with metal lips can be tweaked to one side to change the way the lure tracks.

The procedure employed to make this adjustment is as follows: with a few feet of line out, the angler gives a fast sweep of the pole and watches where the lure goes, an adjustment is made to the hook eye to change the tune, and the lure runs in the opposite direction of the tweak.

Bob Traynor is an expert at tuning lures and can make 10 adjustments to each lure. Goober, on the other hand, thinks everything is great after one pass at tuning and will fish any lure, no matter how ill-tuned or ugly.

Gomer and Goober like to fish on a strict rotation to determine who lands the next fish. Using this system, guests are moved to the head of the rotation because they usually don't get multiple shots at Girthra.

Groovy doesn't like to share his equipment or his spot in the boat. He won't go out unless he's got a good chance to land a fish. This causes some difficulty in the boat. Traynor could not understand why Gomer caught the first fish on Goober's boat as well as the first fish in the St. Larry. Quite simply, Gomer had been up in the rotation on both catches.

Because Bob Traynor did not agree with the rotation system, a modification was proposed so that Bob fished his rod and Goober, Gomer, and the guest rotated the other two rods. The caveat was that the last person to catch a fish was moved to the middle position, acknowledged to be the least productive position. (Gomer's boat ought to fly Gomer's flag, and the flag officer is God on the water, but Gomer and Goober always made special adjustments for a guy who has the ear of Musky Bill.)

On the evening in question, Goober was working the two shared rods in the cockpit, which put him in the middle and starboard side positions. Gomer was driving the boat, picking the route, and watching for traffic that might require an alteration of the course. Gomer also had to read the depth finder, as water that is too skinny will allow Davy Jones to snatch a lure. (Traynor is of the opinion that if he loses a lure to Davy Jones, the driver owes him a lure or money to replace his loss.) Groovy was camped out in the port corner, ready to strike his rod. As the guest, Stock Boy was wondering whether Groovy would give him a shot at a fish in his corner.

Unfortunately, Goober put out an untuned lure in the middle just before Gomer made a wicked turn to the right, and in short order both of the shared lines were tangled. Luckily, Gomer and Goober carry extra setups and two new lines were let out. Gomer must have been going in circles at this point because he turned right again. Goober put out the same untuned lure and tangled two more lines.

Gomer and Goober had a fifth pole, which was sent out in the middle with a different lure. This was also an untuned lure, but it ran out the other direction and tangled with Groovy's line. It was at this point, with no lines left to put in the water and after a thorough cussing from Gomer and much rolling of the eyes by Groovy, that Goober finally agreed to only put out lures that were in tune.

Later, when they were discussing a Roth IRA, Goober told Stock Boy that he didn't tune his lures very much because he couldn't see them in the water and, because of a bum shoulder, couldn't get a good sweep through the water anyway. Goober always has an excuse.

Chapter Three

NOW, FOR A CHECK OF THE SCOREBOARD

SAYINGS NUMBER 33 AND 34

Only Orange Bellies Will Work/Pinch

Their Tails for a Measurement

Groovy Traynor had more lures than Gomer and Goober combined (They did combine their lures, moving them from boat to boat). This imbalance was slowly being rectified as Goober was on the budget plan and was trying to build up his tackle box. He was commenting one day about what happened when he went to Bart's Fishing Crib to purchase a few lures. Goober moved around in his work, and on the occasions when he drove near Bart's, he sometimes stopped in to buy a few lures.

"I pulled up to Bart's and saw Traynor's car there as I walked into the store. I went straight for the musky lures," he explained.

Bart's Fishing Crib is the premier musky lure source in the entire straits area. Traynor wasn't on the lazy bench up front but back in the rod and reel section, according to Goober

"Groovy soon came up and started telling me which colors were the hot ones that I should buy. He looked at the three jointed crank baits in my hand and said that one of them was the hot lure." Goober was talking and Stock Boy listened intently.

"I took the hot lure and returned it to the display and selected a different one."

"That'd be my second or third choice, but it's still a hot one," Groovy said when he saw the exchange.

"Groovy was telling me this from his vast experience, which consisted of some preseason slaughter and a dedicated program of sucking up knowledge from musky men," Goober said.

This was another area where Traynor's real skill was at inflating himself and his achievement. He constructed an artificial self by tearing down others, especially his long-standing friends. Goober went on about his shopping trip.

"I'm sometimes sort of a contrary individual, and the process of him instructing and me rejecting took a few more repetitions before I had three lures that Groovy didn't recommend yet I liked. I bought them and didn't hear more on the subject." Goober paused before continuing.

"Later in the season, I bought a particular crank bait that had a discontinued pattern. Groovy didn't see it until I sent it out for a troll one Wednesday, and he had a good laugh at what a stupid person I was to try this lure. When I beefed him about laughing at me, he said that Nibblytch caught his big one on that pattern."

Goober knew that real musky guides don't let their disdain for inexperienced anglers show. "This guy, one-upping me, laughs behind my back. Incidentally, customized as a member of the BHA, that lure caught two fish and was claimed by Davy Jones before it could grab Girthra."

"Another lure, which I bought from a dealer other than Bart, didn't pass muster with Groovy when I let it out for the first time," Goober continued.

"'Why did you buy that? I could have told you only orange bellies will work on these crank baits. You should've let me show you.' Groovy was gonna straighten me out," Goober smiled.

"I told him, 'I'll decide what lure I'll buy, Bob.'" Goober said. He went on.

"The season progressed, and the lure without the orange belly caught one fish in August. Some of these muskellunge come in like Styrofoam logs. There is no fight and you can just reel them in and let them loose without them seeming to notice. Anyway, this non-fighting 30-inch male musky was all that the lure without the orange belly had caught when October rolled around," Goober said.

"Then the pariah lure caught the best fish ever to be landed on *Mr. 88* . There is film footage of the 50-incher that the lure pulled in. It is shown to outreach a 48-inch straightedge, and if one listens to the soundtrack on the film, I can be heard in the background yipping to Groovy about how they won't work without the orange belly," said Goober.

That's the biggest fish over the transom on *Mr. 88* since Gomer has owned it. The pretend runner-up to the all-time winner of the Snooky Cup (Best fish of the season between Gomer, Goober, and Groovy) is a supposed 49-incher that Groovy caught with his brother Donny.

In a 17-foot Smoker Craft, they brought in their fish at night, and Donny measured it, like a striper, just to the vee in the tail. Only after they'd done a clean release did Groovy tell Donny, "Pinch their tales for a measurement." That's probably why Groovy thinks he should be Goober's guide from hell. Other than that fish with his brother, who is inexperienced with muskies, Groovy hasn't even been able to lie his way into the top spot for the all-time Snooky cup.

Either Gomer or Goober can land and release a musky with aplomb, while Groovy is afraid to touch the fish. One time, for the tagging of a live release, Groovy was afraid to lift up the dorsal fin where the tag is placed, even though Goober had control of the fish. Another time, while Goober was holding up the fish and Groovy was trying to remove the hooks, the following exchange took place.

"Traynor, get the pliers and get this one hook out so we can release this guy."

"I can't find the pliers. Oh, here they are." Groovy moved up to within three or four feet of the fish with a pair of 10-inch-long needle-nosed pliers and reached out to grab the hook. Instead of backing the hook out through the hole it created when it went in, Groovy tried to just give a big yank and get it loose. That didn't work so he gave another big yank. All the while, he was reaching with arms outstretched, head turned, and feet ready to run, and had little control of the pliers.

"You dumb ass: you had one hook to get out, and now you've got three more hooks in him. We gotta get the fish back in the water," Goober said. He was getting pretty aggravated when Gomer grabbed the pliers and promptly unhooked the fish.

Some doubt any tales Groovy tells about handling of fish by himself because he is, so obviously, afraid of any such situation. Essentially, the only job in the landing and release sequence that can be reliably entrusted to Groovy is holding the spotlight.

Chapter Four

OLD GROANER AND GIRTHRA

SAYING NUMBER 35
That Bogagrip is Too Short

The muskellunge has a lure for the fisherman different from that of any other freshwater fish. The bass man searches for the 10-pounder, chuckin', flippin', and duckin' his way through thousands of fish. The walleye fisherman eats his way toward a 15-pounder spring, summer, and fall. The trouter seeks the cold purity of remote waters.

The musky man is different.

Wisconsin and New York have traditionally competed for the reputation as the top musky areas in the United States. Ontario has a naturally reproducing population of muskies and shares these populations in the St. Larry and the straits area with New York State.

Some say it is the remote, beautiful stretches of water that draw people to the musky. However, the Upper Straits area is quite settled and industrialized and very productive. The Nehi Canal at the old steel plant, with its warm water discharge, is an attractant to muskies and their hunters. The place is ugly, stinky, dirty, noisy, and full of big fish. The departure of the last vestiges of the steel industry has now made it not so stinky or noisy.

Some say it is the position of the fish at the top of the fresh-water food chain that draws anglers to muskies. It's like the thrill of knocking over the king of the hill; that's possible and part of it. But it's also the work, the perceived danger, the harsh conditions, the hunting, the determination, the learning, and, always, the chance for a bigger fish.

Both Wisconsin and New York claim world record muskies approaching 70 pounds. Wisconsin claims New York's record is bogus. New York still considers it legitimate. There are also rumors of conservation officers catching 80- or even 100-pound muskies in nets. There have been sightings of huge fish thought to be muskies. Those could be sturgeon.

No one knows how big muskies can get.

There is no doubt about one thing, though: the really big fish are the breeding females. Muskies need a large body cavity to produce the prodigious number of eggs laid during spawning season. The males are generally smaller and not long-lived enough to reach the monster sizes of the trophy females.

Fifty inches is considered trophy size. Weight and girth then become important measurements after that trophy length is reached or exceeded. There are formulas that use length and girth to calculate weight. Phooey to that. There is too much variation in individual muskies to put any stock into anything but a weight on a good scale.

During a single week last year, Gomer and Goober caught a 45-, 46-, and 44-incher, with the last being obviously heavier and fatter than the two longer ones preceding it. Likewise, Gomer and Goober have caught "pinhead" fish, where the body seems outsized in comparison to the head. These are actually normal heads on large bodies, which make for a heavier weight.

Catching this energetic wild animal to measure it, weigh it, girth it, take a few photos, and release it unscathed is a daunting task. At 50 inches, the fish could weigh 40 pounds, and she can spin herself around when she is completely out of the water.

Muskies have large, very sharp teeth—teeth that are scary enough without a 10-inch lure with three razor-sharp treble hooks in their mouths. Their gill plates are covered in sharp edges, which can rake exposed flesh. The heavy-gauge leader is like a wire saw to hold. If she is boated with a conventional net, the hooks get all enmeshed in the net, and one can't get them out quickly or easily. The accuracy of any measurement under these conditions is questionable.

The only accurate measurements are those taken when a fish is killed or kept out of the water an inordinately long time. Catch-and-release operations are best done by two or three experienced anglers, working quickly and as a team. Since many musky anglers are men, they are extremely concerned with comparing how long their fishes are. This competitiveness makes the more experienced anglers trophy hunters. The act of trophy fishing makes trophies unlikely if the potential trophies are kept and killed.

The big one everyone is after is female, she is heavy, and she is named Girthra in lore. On the way to take Girthra, anglers are going to catch a great number of smaller muskies. Many of these will be males, and they will show signs of the kind of lives muskies lead. Early in the season, during the post-spawning period, the fish are weary, and some of them are battle scarred. It is not uncommon to find the males covered with scratches and scrapes as well as lamprey bites.

Goober's daughter once caught a musky that was so scraped up on the sides that it looked as if it had been run over by a lawnmower. Commonly, fins show signs of wear against the gravel of the spawning beds. As the season goes on, the battle scars diminish in most cases. Then, instead of fighting to breed, they are competing for food. Muskies eat everything, including each other.

Last year, Johnny Lawrence of the Straits Musky Club netted a 32-inch musky flopping around on the surface with a 26-inch musky in his mouth. A 52-incher killed a few years back had a 36-inch musky in her belly. Life is tough for a musky and doubly so for the males, it seems.

One night in the early fall of '97, Gomer and Goober were on their endless troll. They were using the new boat, which is slightly smaller than their stealth machine, because neither Floyd nor Otis nor Aunt Flo nor Ernest T nor any of the guys down at the Noco station had come along. Gomer and Goober hadn't scared up any muskies in the past few days. As summer faded away, there were fewer pleasure boaters and rocketeers ("rocketeer" is derived from the slang name "crotch rocket" and is used for those who ride jet skis or personal watercraft) on the water. There are numerous shoreline lights in the Upper Straits, and sometimes the sky doesn't really get completely dark. The dark came early at that time of year, around seven o'clock.

Gomer and Goober had been trolling their rotation of different colors of customized crank baits for a few hours when they got a good strike and fought a 42-inch male to the boat. Though Gomer and Goober try to follow the sayings of Musky Bill, they screw up as often as not. Being a couple of doofuses, Gomer and Goober didn't realize that Musky Bill had a saying that was relevant that particular night: "That Bogagrip is too short." The Bogagrip is a tool for gripping the lip of toothy fish in order to land it with no harm to fish or fisherman. Gomer and Goober were the only members of the Straits Musky Club to use the Bogagrip at that time, most members being too cheap to buy the tool and preferring instead to use the less expensive and illegal gaff. Gomer boated the battle-scarred veteran neatly with the Bogagrip. Inside the boat, with such light as they could pick up, they let the fishing line go slack to remove the hooks.

Goober began to measure the length and said, "Hey Gomer, look at this!"

Two-thirds of the way down the fish's port side, a chunk of flesh as big as a man's fist had been bitten out. The wound was largely healed over, although the scaling in the area was spotty. "Hey Goober, look at this!"

The fish's starboard eye was a milky marble, obviously totally blind. "Look what else Gomer: three lamprey bites on his belly."

Within a few seconds, they got some still pictures of this fish, released him alive, and dubbed him Old Groaner. Old Groaner had lived through quite a bit to get to 42 inches, and he went back into the straits alive, a symbol of perseverance to males everywhere.

One is not halfway to the quest for Girthra when he has released a battered male like Old Groaner. There are many Old Groaners on the Quest for Girthra using the lore of Musky Bill.

Chapter Five

STEALTH TECHNOLOGY

SAYINGS NUMBER 36 AND 37

Sharpen Your Hooks/Don't Take a Chance on Old Line

Gomer was 46 years old and had been boating for 38 years, at least. His father had a summer place in Ontario, and his brothers and he would always take over his Dad's boats. Gomer's father, Clem, would buy a bigger and slower boat each year so that it would be less attractive to his boys. They were summer boaters in small open boats. Gomer has done all the foolish things boys will do because "boys is boys." Along the way, he's learned a few things about boating.

Editor's note: Gomer is famous for having perfected the Bat Turn between bridge pylons, a maneuver that cost his father some of those boats.

The most important piece of musky gear is the boat, and one spends money on it that a guy like Groovy Traynor spends on lures, GoreTex, candy, or Schnapps.

That is how the stealth technology came about. Through Traynor freeloading off other guys, word came back to Gomer that he wasn't visible at night. His green and red lights were not being picked up by other boats, and that rendered him invisible. That tidbit of news and his radio silence became known as stealth technology. Because his boat is larger than most musky boats on the Strait, the green and red lights are on the sides and up off the deck. On smaller boats, the lights are next to each other on the bow. The other boats were looking for the lights in the wrong place. Enhancing the stealth approach was the effect observed when they turned on the floodlight and suddenly appeared to materialize where they hadn't been just moments before.

One day, when Goober and Gomer were waiting for Groovy, Goober said, "You know that Musky Bill says, 'Sharpen your hooks,'" as he ground away at one.

"I've got an idea," Gomer said as he rummaged in the electrical parts box. "I'm going to replace the bulbs in my side lights with low-wattage ones just to get Traynor going."

"Hey, Gom, do you think that's safe?"

"They claim they can't see me now, so what's the difference?"

Goober continued to sharpen as they waited for Traynor to show, and Gomer quickly rebulbed the navigation lights. When Groovy showed up, Goober asked him what he'd been doing.

"Nothing much. I made all new leaders with my wire crimper and sleeves, and I sharpened the hooks on my confidence baits."

"Gomer installed stealth technology while I tried to live up to the sayings of Musky Bill by sharpening some hooks," Goober replied.

Groovy wouldn't ask what stealth technology was, and it took several weeks for him to find out.

Here's why Goober is such a goober: he's willing, but he ain't always able. One year, they were launching Gomer's boat at the marina using Goober's truck. Gomer was driving, and Goobs was spotting. They had to wait for a guy with two young ladies with him to clear the slip. Goober took a boat hook and waited on the dock.

The guy was having some difficulty getting going. Meanwhile, the two ladies stripped off their jeans and shirts down to their bathing suits. This activity riveted Goober's attention.

Meanwhile, back at the launch, Gomer had moved forward

to get a straighter shot at the slip. Then he backed himself to the top of the ramp. But when he stopped backing up, the trailer kept moving. He flew out of the truck and grabbed the tongue of the trailer just before it went over to the steep part of the ramp.

The guys at dock two, who were watching this, said it was even money whether Gomer could stop the boat or not. He dug his heels in, yelled for Goober, and held on as the 4-ton boat slowly stopped rolling. Gomer's heels plowed a couple of furrows in the gravel.

Goober finally came up the ramp as Gomer stopped the boat and said, "Need any help?"

A few years back, there was a musky slaughter in June where 13 fish over 50 inches and 56 over 30 pounds were caught on opening day. It was a truly amazing day.

When Goober and Gomer went to the St. Larry, it was a lure slaughter. Advice from everyone, except Musky Bill, said to fish deep. Goober put on Believers. The bottom took them. Goober put on the Hooker. The bottom took him. Goober put on Jondier lures. The bottom got them. The leaders got shredded. The 50-pound test broke. After the first day, they slacked off a bit in the lure slaughter and found out that charts and the advice of Musky Bill, "Don't take a chance on old line," were very helpful.

They don't call them Gomer and Goober for nothing.

Chapter Six

DAVY AND GOMER

Saying Number 38

Only Fish with Someone You Can Count On

If you remember your tenth-grade earth science, you know that a strait is a narrow body of water that connects two larger bodies of water. The straits we speak of in the lore of Musky Bill is big water itself because it connects two very big bodies of water. The size of the Musky Straits has caused it to be mislabeled throughout history as the Musky River. In fact, the famous cascade at the straits has caused people to mislabel the Musky River as two rivers—the Upper Musky and the Lower Musky. The cascade at the straits is commonly known as Musky Falls.

Though thought of as a haven for honeymooners, Musky Falls has a much darker history as a magnet for suicides. Davy is the owner of Davy Jones' locker, which is the repository of all things dropped overboard in ocean or lake. Davy also beckons the unwise, unwary, suicidal, foolish, stupid, and unlucky to the Musky River and Musky Falls.

And Davy gets who he is after. He gets the inexperienced boaters who miss their marina. He gets the three lawyers who thought it would be a lark to walk across the ice. He gets the kayaker who thought he could paddle fast enough to escape the flow over the cascades. He gets the fishermen who fail to turn their lights on at night. He gets the hard worker who tries to rescue a sliding snow blower. He gets the drunk who walks off the end of the dock. He gets a few every year. Before the white man came to the Musky River, he got the legendary Native American maiden. Davy even gets people trying to reach his grasp who never make it, such as the lovelorn redneck who tried dashing across eight lanes of rush-hour traffic to throw himself into the straits, only to be bounced from car to car until he slid down the bank and ended half in the water of the canal that parallels the straits.

But Davy doesn't get everybody whom he seems destined to grab. The Musky Falls Park Police and intrepid firefighters have rescued children from the brink of the cascade as well as those who were clinging to rocks in sight of the edge. Others have scuttled their boats on the rocks just before Davy's invisible hand reached out to snatch them. When a few inexperienced boaters anchored their boat from the rear, the current quickly dragged down the stern and began to fill the boat from the back (anchoring your boat in the straits is at least a two-man job, even when done correctly, because the current forces one to drive forward while raising the anchor). Davy Jones was foiled by nearby boaters who rescued the crew before they could be snatched.

Luckily for Goober, foolishness and incompetence are fatal only when Davy is ready for you. Goober is still living proof that Davy Jones is selective as to who and when with his victims. A few years back, Goober and Gomer and Groovy shared ownership of a small fishing boat called the *Pro Bowler*. The *Pro Bowler* was to be used on waters that *Mr. 88* couldn't reach and at times of year when *Mr. 88* was in winter storage. Winter fishing for steelhead entails launching a boat on an icy, slippery dock and the dodging of floating ice during the expedition. The first time Goober took the helm, it was after dark, and he immediately crashed into a sizable chunk of floating ice. The report of the crash was loud enough that the loafers at the docks three-quarters of a mile off heard the noise and asked about it.

When the fellows pulled their boat out of the lower Musky Straits that night, Gomer backed the trailer into the launching area, and Groovy and Goober used ropes to guide the boat onto the trailer. During this procedure, Goober got back in the boat and found himself too far from the dock to just step over from boat to dock. He decided to leap across the gap, and his winter boot hit the icy, slimy, slippery dock. Goober is a sizable guy who is not a total klutz but nevertheless pretty clunky. His boot hit the metal dock edge and slipped. His other boot hit and also slipped. Then, somehow, foot one came back for another try at the edge of the dock. For a few seconds, he looked like a cartoon character whose legs were flailing in midair faster than could be seen. Then, *bang*, his one knee caught the dock and he was able to grab hold and pull himself onto the surface. Though he would only have been in waist deep water at the dock, those were the first two times that Goober dodged the grasp of Davy Jones.

As we have seen earlier, Goober bought a boat a few years back, and since that time he has had several close encounters of the Davy Jones kind. Gomer is an experienced boatman who takes great pains to school Goober in the correct ways to handle, maintain, clean, and care for his new boat. In fact, one of Musky Bill's famous sayings is, "Only fish with someone you can count on." Gomer can be counted on to handle emergencies and usually make good decisions.

With Goober, these traits aren't a certainty. Since he got his boat, Goober has: run his gas tank bone-dry while being swept down-current (his comment: "I wanted to see if my gas gauge was accurate"); spun his prop without a spare or tools to replace it; lost power to both his batteries while fighting the war musky with Aunt Flo; hit bottom in the St. Larry twice because the charts were not equipped with warning alarms (actually, this was done by Gomer once, but both times it was in Goober's boat, and there were several near misses); been nearly pitched into the drink by Aunt Flo while she was rushing her sizable bulk to the same side Goober was on after a hairpin turn; and had Canada jump 10 feet in front of his boat on two different occasions.

There is a long breakwater at the head of the Musky Straits that separates the river from the adjacent Flat Rock Canal. In the early spring, trout are caught on the river side of this breakwall, while the water is still cold enough to have shore ice. Once, when Groovy and Goober were way out on the breakwall, casting for trout, Goober got a snag and went down onto the ice to attempt to free his lure and save his terminal tackle. Groovy was watching from the walkway when a stranger happened along and began to talk with Groovy. Now, Groovy has a good word for everyone and often has many hundreds of good words. He seems to be under the impression that everyone is as interested in hearing him speak as he himself is. He was holding forth to this hapless fellow. Goober moved around trying to free his lure from the rocks or ice or whatever.

"Hey, buddy, you on the ice, you better get back. Where you're standing, there ain't no rocks," the stranger yelled at Goober. Goober scrambled back onto the concrete. He saw the thin ice he'd been on, thanked the stranger, and broke his line. Falling into the straits there with its fast current and icy water would have surely meant that Davy Jones would have gotten him. Goober never did figure out why Groovy didn't mention the thin ice.

People who go out on the *Booster* with Gomer and Goober often wonder why Goober puts up with Gomer being bossy and imperious and sometimes downright mean to Goober on his own boat. Most men bust each other's chops about stuff. The kidding is just good natured. Gomer can go over the line and really aggravate people about sensitive topics at times.

For example, Gomer regularly cracks Goober about the clutter in the cuddy cabin of the *Booster*, though a good percentage of the stuff is his. Gomer beefs Goober about all the recyclable bottles and cans, especially after he overturned a cooler filled with them. In a lot of ways, Gomer is like having a boat-wife, constantly critical and intent on having a bad time about it. Gomer lives an uxorious existence and compensates for this submissiveness to his wife by beating on Goober. What can one expect from someone who traces his lineage to Vlad the Impaler?

Goober knows, however, that even though a cat has only nine lives, Goober has already had 10 or 11 saves from Davy Jones, and without Gomer he might have been sleeping with Davy. The fact that he tells Goober what to do on occasion has been far outweighed by all the saves in maintenance and handling that Gomer has made.

Chapter Seven

KISS MY ROCK

SAYING NUMBER 39

A Musky Hunter Must be Ceremonial

"I don't understand how you can be a rational, intelligent man and still believe in magic." Goober's son offered this opinion.

Father and son were driving along a limited access highway, and Goober had just pointed out a red tailed hawk that crossed their path and said, "Hawk! That will bring good luck."

Goober contemplated this challenge for a few minutes. As a musky man, he did sometimes act in a superstitious manner, but did he really believe in magic?

In the quest for Girthra, the great she-musky of myth, he spent a fair amount of time adapting his practices to those contained in the lore of Musky Bill, as outlined in his List of Forty. One of Musky Bill's sayings is, "A musky hunter must be ceremonial."

Did this require a belief in magic?

"I think, when I see the hawk, or other uncommon wildlife, it means two things that may help me in musky fishing. First, it means the animals, birds, and fishes are active and on the move. Second, it means that I am alert and aware enough to be ready for a conflict with Girthra or one of her entourage. Maybe that is what is meant by the saying, 'God helps man who helps himself.'" Goober's son rolled his eyes and looked at him with an expression that was a mixture of pity and bewilderment that sons reserve for their clueless fathers.

The issue of a musky man being properly ceremonial can take many forms. How Musky Bill's admonition was intended to be demonstrated is cause for constant debate and study. Some musky men see ceremony in the use of a piece of lucky gear (for example, a lucky hat, boots, or lure). Some see it in a small celebration after a catch. For example, Groovy has been observed kissing a smooth rock, said to be from Grandfather's Island, which is kept in his tackle box. After a fish has been caught, he offers a nip of Schnapps all around. Groovy also likes a personal dose of Schnapps at times when he feels no one is looking. (Of course, with Groovy, it's rotgut Schnapps for sharing and imported German stuff for personal consumption.)

Musky ceremonies can be conducted pre-fish or post-fish. They can involve prayers and incantations, burning of substances of magical significance, smoking of tobacco in special rituals, activities such as the little musky dance for one or more anglers, or other things too weird to imagine.

Goober and Aunt Flo use the council of war ceremonial. In a council of war, the lowest-ranking officer speaks first, each successive rank speaks next, until the highest-ranking individual speaks last and makes the decision. On a ceremonial basis, Goober and Flo hold councils after the first run and then after every third run thereafter. This is how they decide to continue what they are doing or alter their pattern.

Ceremonies require maintenance. Neglect of them shows a lack of concentration and, subsequently, no fish. Some musky men believe that the requirement for ceremonial observance leads to monotonously doing the same things over and over. Ceremony reflects concentration and being in tune with the creatures below the surface; it does not replace innovation or new patterns or new runs.

Ritual is the physical manifestation of ceremonial observance. It is different from magic. Magic entails no effort: the wand is waved, the glass slippers are clicked, and good things happen.

Ceremony, however, requires effort. The musky man must be ready physically and mentally, the boat and mind organized, the lines and leaders fresh, everything receptive. When lacking reverence or without proper ceremony, a musky man feels adrift and empty. Observance of ceremonial activities refocuses the mind on the situation at hand.

Musky men can get outlandish with their ceremonial behavior as a result of any number of wacky beliefs. A certain faction of the Straits Musky Club believes that Girthra is *der Geist*, the Great Spirit, or the giant musky that represents the great musky unconscious. It is their doctrine that ceremonial observances above the water are communicated through the wire below the surface to the lair of Girthra, she-musky of Myth. Whether their ceremonies include Schnapps, frappacino, cigars, or other substances, these anglers are adamant that they can breach the watery barrier with their beliefs.

Gomer and Goober have several numerological ceremonies that they conduct to enhance the performance of certain lures. When Gomer went off his rocker one winter and painted and decaled all of Goober's lures, several ended up with the number 20 on them. It came to pass that only the lures with a 20 decal on them caught fish. The best luck occurred when two number 20 lures were out. Hence was born the lore of the twin twenties. Subsequently, one of the original twin twenties became the supreme commander, as it has caught the most fish up to 49 inches. The corner of the boat that catches the most fish has a 20 sticker on the board. Girthra's daughter came off the corner with the 20 sticker. Everyone cheers for a NASCAR driver these days. Goober goes for number 20, Tony Stewart (see The Tony Factor previously). Goober spent time on the waiting list for a boathouse at the marina. When his time came due, it was house number 20 that was available.

The crackpot school systems teach diversity these days. They have drummed it into our kids' heads that there is no difference between legitimate religion and any oddball thing any idiot might dream up. It has gone beyond tolerance to an acceptance of the ridiculous. There is no true musky faith. Odd rituals and pagan ceremonies are a part of musky lore. It isn't just a lucky rabbit's foot or lucky hat but a series of ritualistic actions with a talisman or chanting, singing, and dancing that are observed.

Some musky men like to propose a bet with others to induce the fish to bite. A double loon (a Canadian two-dollar coin valued at around 25 cents US) for the next legal fish is a favorite bet. Some like to take a snort of Schnapps after each successful release. Bob Traynor carries a rock in a velvet pouch in his tackle box. As the boat proceeds toward the fishing grounds, he can be seen rubbing his rock and chanting or praying silently to induce the fish to bite.

As luck is an important aspect of fishing, it seems obvious that "a musky hunter must be ceremonial." Some ceremonies are post-release, wherein the celebrator gives thanks for the success attained. Since musky fishing is not for sustenance, it is hard to believe God cares about which musky hunter can out-brag another. Other ceremonies are pre-expedition, and here, too, they probably don't make it onto God's radar screen. These ritualistic ceremonies do give confidence and satisfaction to the angler and some little concentration prior to his attempt to catch Girthra.

PART FIVE

THE ESCHATON

DREAM ON

Finnegan Mincher's favorite place in the Straits Stretches was named for him, Finnegan Circle at Memory Park. This park was at the highest point in the county, only about 1,000 feet above sea level, but it was out where the local television stations had their broadcast towers. Finn liked to walk his dogs around the half-mile-long circle. He could keep track of laps and regulate his exercise.

On this day, he parked the truck, hooked up his beasts, and looked up to see an old motorcycle with Rear Admiral Gid and another man on board. Instead of helmets, they wore cloth caps like WWI biplane aces had worn. Finn was a little taken aback when they roared off with a whoop and a holler around the circle.

The dogs didn't notice the people or the noise, and Finn began to walk them. He had gone about an eighth of the way around the circle when he came upon his father, standing next to the Indian motorcycle, hat unstrapped, and wearing a shirt that said "Otto" over the left breast. Gid Gunmore was gone.

"Hello, son," said Otto Conrad. Otto had been his father's nickname, not his given name. Finn had failed to connect the outlines from Otto Conrad with his memories of his father. His father, who had never been a musky fisherman, had passed away 7 years before. Finn was nonplussed.

"You've been behind all these messages?"

"A channel to you from someone you had in your unconscious mind." He nodded.

"Maybe you can explain some of the stuff to me now." The dogs were pulling at their leashes and turning their heads sideways, shaking their ears, and giving little whines. To them, Finn was talking to himself.

"You've seen the last of Gid, and today you'll see the last of me. The story of the quest for Girthra ends with this installment. You will still have many questions. There will always be things you can't know. You will move on. There are more dreams to come. Now you understand, the quest is not for big fish; it is for moral virtue."

Moral virtue, Finn thought. So that's what it all boiled down to. The body-slams that hit a man in his life—downsizing, scornful children, spouses that no longer even tolerated you—could all be regretted without affecting the *ding an sich*, the thing in itself. The man was who he was. All these things had made him, and there was more to come, Finn realized.

Finn let the dogs off their leashes. They ran off in a game of tag that apparently amused them intensely and gave Finn a feeling of appreciation for the beauty of the world. Finn tells his sister-in-law that his dog's name was Iroquois for "Runs in Beauty."

Finn would regret the end of these chats with Gid, but he straightened his shoulders and felt ready to complete his quest. A man needs to make decisions, overcome the wrong ones and move on to a new challenge. He'd seen many men with nothing on their agenda but dying to get it over with.

Finn glanced back to Otto just in time to see him ride off on the Indian and dissolve into a cloud. Once again, Finn looked down to find he had the usual sheet of notes and thin chapter in his hand.

He sat at a picnic table while the dogs romped, complete in their happiness. Finn allowed his mind to wander.

A skeleton of a musky had washed up on the floor of the boathouse with other debris when the water had risen 5 feet while Finn was away. He had been away helping out his brother's family in a southern state after his niece had broken her back. He kept his musky skull hanging on the boathouse wall.

Things had been falling into place for Finny Minny for several years. Coincidences, visions, epiphanies; he couldn't decide what they were. He'd been assigned boathouse number 20 after being on a waiting list for several years. Twenty was his lucky number. Two twenties were especially lucky, and the corner of his boat with the 20 sticker on the musky board and a lure with a number 20 decal on it were the combination that yielded the biggest fish. Was Finn losing his mind or going with the flow?

After walking his dogs, Finnegan Mincher opened the final volume of the story.

RICHARD A. MINICH

*A dream of the death of Girthra. Otto Conrad's news of Goober's epic
struggle. Goober lands atop the musky world in 5 years.*

Bull of heaven brings on plagues and disasters
Confrontation with our own morality
7 collective hero
numerology mimic revelations using same numbers
in a musky context
1... God
2... Society
3... Heavenly (Trinity)
4... Earth, Compass Points, Worldly
5... Man, Imperfection
6... Evil, incompleteness, moral corruption
7... Perfection, Heaven and Earth, 3+4
12...Harmony
20...Halfway to Completion
40...Completion
*Girthra begat seven daughters to the four corners of the musky world,
12 granddaughters to the seven great musky habitations, and 40 great
granddaughters to inhabit the musky universe, from which sprung
the 144,000 muskies*

"

The gods destroy the heroes with a sudden blow,
but they grind the mediocrities for weary, weary, years."
Robertson Davies

"This is the Great Theater of Life. Admission is free but the taxation
is mortal. You come when you can, and leave when you must.
The show is continuous."
Ibid

"I am not a down-and-out asking God for a handout when I kneel;
I am offering something, I am making a gift, a gift of myself, and the
beauty and order of the ceremonial are the outward forms in which this
mutuality of affection, offering, and trust are made possible."

Ibid
Otto Conrad

Chapter One

GOOBER SHOCKS THE MUSKY CLUB

SAYING NUMBER 40

Whatever You've Got, There's a Musky that Can Defeat It!

"I think I'll take it in this corner," Goober told Snooky, "Well, maybe not."

"That's a big fish!" Snooky shouted.

They were on their first pass on the CBGB run. Though musky lore says to fish the new moon, and particularly moonset on the new moon, Goober and Snooky, Goober and Aunt Flo, Goober and Groovy, and Goober and Gomer usually just went when they could.

Today, Goober and Snooky had hit it just right. A new moon with moonset and sunset within minutes of each other. It was warm for October. It was calm and nobody was fishing, maybe one other boat. They were on one of Slim Tomkins' runs. Slim is a charter captain specializing in musky on the Upper Musky Straits. On the shore side of the boat, they had a perch bait running at a depth of about 24 feet. On the sea side, they had a Depth Raider at about 18 feet. This combination meant that the deeper lure would come along ticking the bottom first while the suspended lure was 40 or 50 feet behind.

A structure on the bottom caused the shore-side rod to crash and bang as it tried to hurry around the curve that the boat was taking. The sea-side rod alternated between floating upward on a slack line and sudden pulls, which caused it to dart about. The boat had just straightened out, after coming around the bend, when the sea-side rod went off.

The reel screamed without letup: it sounded like they'd snagged the bottom. Goober eased off the throttle and readied to turn into the snag when Snooky yelled, "Fish on, and it's a big one!"

Goober and Snooky each fished their own rods, and Goober fished the 20 corner that had his Tony Stewart NASCAR number 20 sticker on it. Therefore, when Snooky lifted the rod and felt the fish rather than a snag, it was Goober who shifted the boat to neutral and fought his fish.

The deep-diving lures used in musky fishing will reach their maximum depth or hit bottom with little line out. This lure had about 120 feet out, a long line for trolling crankbaits because of their diving lips, and the big fish swam straight toward the boat. Snooky barely had time to clear the other rod and gather up the release tools, net, ultra-long-nosed pliers, hook-cutter, and tagging gun before the Boomer loomed along beside the boat.

She saw Goober and quickly peeled off about 20 feet of line. Goober was used to this reaction: in his younger days, girls had recoiled at the sight of him in a similar fashion. It didn't take long for this musky to be heading back toward the net, however, because the combination of the slight current from the Pantherville River and the light waves from the Upper Lake slowly turned the boat in the direction the fish was swimming. Goober reeled as fast as he could to keep the line from going slack. As the fish came alongside, the size of her became obvious.

"That fish is huge!" said Snooky.

"Let's do this right. Take the rod and give me the net." Goober extended his rod to Snooky and reached out for the net with his free hand. "She's coming right for us!" he added.

He noticed that only one hook of the last of the three trebles on the Depth Raider was in her mouth. Snooky reeled down to the leader, stepped backward, and Goober came in with the net. She swam right in, and Goober scooped her rather easily.

With one hook in her mouth, she was in the net. One shake and that hook would have been gone. When examining the lure later, it was found that the hook hanger for the rear hook was blown out. If that lure had failed seconds earlier, the big fish would just be a tall tale. The heroic musky hunters would not have believed the story.

The boat had drifted toward the cityscape while Goober had been fighting the fish. Snooky had to deftly but slowly reverse the boat to keep it from drifting into a buoy. Now they had to get this monster measured, photographed, revived, and released.

The first lift of this wild animal caught Goober in the back. He had tried to grab tail and gill raker and lift with his arms. He could not do it. He knew he had to lift the 50-pounder with his knees.

This proved equally impossible because his feet lifted off the deck as soon as he leaned over the gunwale and tried lifting the fish. Snooky had to grab his legs like a linebacker making a tackle to keep him from going overboard. Finally, both Snooky and Goober had to grab the net and hoist the fish over the side. Goober quickly lined up the measuring stick.

"57!" he yelled.

"She's not lined up. What now?" Snooky asked.

"53!"

"Let's get a picture and get her back in the water!"

The release was the most important part for Goober. He got a hand inside her jaws from underneath, without touching her gills, and used his other arm to cradle a huge stomach. Bending his knees, he was able to stand, although he had exerted himself. The first photo, famously known as the egg picture, clearly shows the grimace of strain caused by the weight of this monster musky.

Snooky said, "Smile, you're having fun."

Goober was thinking, "How do I put this fish in the water without straining my back or losing a non-revived fish overboard?" Goober is no longer a stout enough fellow to reach out with one arm and hold 50 pounds under control, but he found a back-saving maneuver to release Girthra's granddaughter.

He slid his arm down and grabbed the area just above the tail. That area proved too large to clasp without excessive strain and rapid cramping. He also had his right hand in the area under the gill covers. (Goober would tell the tale in the future of the noise made when he grabbed this fish under the jaw. He'd say, "It went '*errrk*,' just like my dog. She had the same expression as my dog, and she even weighed about the same as him—56 pounds.").

Using the gunwale as a fulcrum and his body as the lever, Goober kept his back straight, counted on Snooky to hold his legs to prevent him from toppling into the water, and laid the huge horse back into the waters of the Upper Lake. Once the fish touched the water, the weight was off Goober's back, and he could kneel down and pump the tail to aerate the fish's gills.

In a very few minutes, he had to call on Snooky for relief, as his hand was cramping on the tail. They made three attempts to tag the fish, but the area to be tagged, the dorsal fin, just shrugged off the tags because they were too small. After Snooky revived her with each hand, she was ready to swim lazily away.

She headed right for the *Croaker*, an old submarine moored for display nearby. She looked like a submarine as she slowly sank out of sight while moving away.

No measure of girth had been made; no weight had been taken. Snooky and Goober looked around at the end of their release to see if anyone had seen what just happened. JohnJohn and Clem appeared to be nearby but too far away to have witnessed the adventure.

Goober reported the fish as tagged the next day, without comment. A few days later, he posted a photograph on the Straits Musky Club email list with the comment, "53 inches. Is this 50 pounds?"

Simon Anthony, noted musky snob, made no reply. Ike Borodino, heroic musky man, commented that it was 46 pounds.

Goober had posted three pictures, each taken in succession. The first was the musky egg, where the fish's tail was curled around Goober and only its hugely fat belly showed. The fish appeared to have eaten a pot-bellied pig just prior to capture. The second picture showed the fish with Goober grimacing and the fish beginning to slide down his chest. The third, in which Goober smiles, shows the fish farther down his chest.

The *Booster* had landed three monster fish in 12 months in the one-mile stretch from Mr. T's pilings to Girthra's weedbed to CBGB.

This 53-incher had Goober feeling elated for days.

Goober was thankful for Snooky being along on this run because he had tried to bring a very large musky to boat by himself earlier in the season, and the landing had been a difficult one. It was exhausting to Goober and dangerous to the fish. When catching big muskies, it's best to get them to boatside directly; long fights are discouraged. Light tackle can exhaust the musky to the point of death. When the lone fisherman has the fish beside the boat, the rod goes into a rod holder and the huge musky net is used to corral the beast. With two people, one can handle the rod and one the net. The person with the rod reels up to the leader and walks backward in the boat while the netter ducks under his line and scoops up the fish.

What had happened to Goober when he was solo was that every time he tried to set the rod aside, the fish pulled out more line against the drag and Goober had to reel her in again. When he finally had his net in hand and tried to scoop the fish, he caught the lure on the leading edge of the net's basket but did not have the fish in the net. He was able to get her in the net eventually by turning the net inside out under the fish. That is a hard task with a net that has a basket 48 inches in diameter.

Goober finally got the fish in the net, but both fish and net were firmly hooked. Unhooking muskies is always treacherous because they can do uncanny acrobatics and do them so fast that one cannot see their movements. You can look up endless stories of stunts muskies have performed while being unhooked and released. Muskies have been brought to the boat having eaten the lure endwise, with nine hooks in the mouth and the mouth thereby hooked shut, only to flip a couple of times, all the hooks are suddenly out of the fish, and the lure has somehow hooked the angler's shirt or hand.

In order to work on removing the lure, Goober had to put down the net. This net, if it went overboard, would sink like an anchor and drag the musky down with it. Goober used a bungee cord to secure the net to the boat and grabbed for his long-nosed pliers to remove the hooks from the edge of the net. In an ordinary net, snagging the netting catches the hooks and winds them up, making removal almost impossible to accomplish quickly. The specialized musky nets have a coating on the netting to resist catching the hooks. Giant nets are the preferred way to land muskies and are required on really big fish. So, with the fish in the water, Goober was able to remove the hooks from the fish's mouth.

The previous year, Goober had learned the limits of his Bogagrip on a 48-inch fish caught by Gomer. The Bogagrip is a lip-holding device that holds the fish 6 inches from the hand holding the Boga. When the 48-incher, thought to be secure in the grip, did a mid-air spin, it bent the jaws enough to fall back into the water. Big fish require the net. When the fish is in the net and no hooks are around, one can get his hand under the jaw and lift the fish into the air, grabbing the body just above the tail with his other hand to get a few quick photos snapped by the fishing partner.

Problems increase with size. As the fish go up to and over 50 inches long, a musky geezer's ability to lift 40 or 45 or even 50 pounds of wild animal with one hand while leaning over the water comes into question. The Straits Musky Club spends a great deal of time and energy trying to convince everyone to handle muskies correctly and carefully. This effort is important and undoubtedly saves the lives of some muskies. However, these fish are big enough to break anything you've got, including your wrist and or arm. Remember, "whatever you've got, there's a musky that can defeat it."

As soon as you touch the musky, your hands are covered with slime, and everything you touch slips out of your hands. By the time Goober had the 50-incher that he caught solo beside the boat for revival, he was both elated and whipped. Through his exhaustion he looked around to see if any nearby boats had noticed his struggle, but no boats were nearby when he looked. Each time he looked back down to concentrate on pumping the fish, he heard the happy voices of children at summer play.

Later, when Goober alerted the club via email that he'd caught a whopper, Simon Anthony and Ike Borodino explained to him in return emails that he couldn't have caught that fish at that time, with that method, or in that place unless he'd had at least 10 years' experience.

Chapter Two

COMIN' 'ROUND THE CORNER

CROSSING THE WATERS OF DEATH

They had waited two full days after the big blow, when the lake had risen to 18- to 24-foot or larger waves for a full day. Melvin Loonch and Bob Traynor knew the lake would still be plenty muddy, but that is where the giant fish are. Musky men need big fish for their self-esteem.

So, they went south down the Musky Straits into Canada, with the hope of sneaking behind the breakwaters and catching Girthra or one of her daughters. It's tricky to pick up how high the waves are crashing as one heads down the straits. The waves on the reefs to the east always show some white. When one glimpses them breaking over the west breakwater, it begins to get worrisome.

Groovy and Goober were cautious as Loonch poked the bow of his 25-foot boat out past the channel buoy's spot. Those wacky Canadians had pulled their buoys about 5 weeks earlier. He relied on his GPS to confirm that he was approaching the place on the charts that signifies the opening into the lake. Here, the big rollers from two days ago still contained plenty of energy, 5- to 7-footers with long wavelengths of 25 to 30 feet.

A word or two about boats: nobody uses flat-bottom bass boats on the Upper Lake other than during a few days in the summer. The Upper Lake is treacherous and famous for wrecking all kinds of boats since the time when the Europeans began coming to America.

Most of the musky men use semi-vee or deep-vee aluminum boats that they launch behind the breakwaters on a trailer. This obviates the need to come around the corner of the breakwall and expose themselves to the Upper Lake's fury.

The boat Goober drives is a 25-foot fiberglass sport fisher built for the ocean off Florida. It's warmer, safer, more stable, and stronger than the usual musky boat, but it's not easy to trailer. It stays in a slip all season down on the straits. It must brave the waters at the head of the straits to get to where the big fish can be found.

They eased her out into the Lake and once past the channel buoy were able to turn east with the push of the southwest wind mostly behind them. They moved toward the north end of the west breakwater. Having such big waves behind one's boat is unnerving, even if one has felt it before; it's as if a giant hand has cradled the back of the boat and is prepared to fling it forward. Looking back, the waves are above your head and look as if they will bury the boat with the next push. Of course, the boat floats, and the wave doesn't crash over the transom. But it feels better to get behind the breakwaters and receive the protection offered.

That day, Gomer and Goober fished a number of their runs at both ends of the protected area but were unable to coax a bite from the muddy water. As the hours rolled along, they often looked at the breaking waves. The waves had started the day coming over the walls and were still doing so after 6 hours of fishing. The storm was a few days old, the wind was mild and lowering, and the weather channel had indicated the waves would be subsiding. Loonch is an optimist and thought they would have lessened in 6 hours.

He was wrong as they headed for home.

There are two ways to return to the boat slip: through the lock and canal, or around the corner. Around the corner is faster by at least an hour and preferred on most occasions. As Goober piloted the boat out from behind the west breakwater, he met those real waves that had come from the southwest all the way down the length of the Upper Lake. Those 5- to 7-footers of the morning had now become 10- to 12- footers. Their wavelength had shortened, too.

The situation was dangerous; it was approaching the limits of what boat and pilot were capable of doing. From the north end of the west breakwater to the channel head is 77 one-hundredths of a mile, according to the GPS. It is important to get as far as where the channel buoy belongs. A failure to go far enough west has brought numerous boats to grief, on the middle reefs and other rocky spots, over the years. Once one gets around that buoy, the mass of Canada begins to offer some relief from the push, and that giant, invisible hand settles under the transom and propels one forward.

It's just that three-quarters of a mile that is the problem.

Captain Coop and Goober had been around the corner in worse waves than these, but Coop had been driving. Not only had they had waves breaking over the bow, but they'd even had a few come over the top. A well-designed boat with a good top will shed most of the water instantly from such waves. An open-bow design would fill up and require the pumps to work hard to keep from becoming swamped. Luckily, that was not Gomer and Goober's problem.

Having watched Coop use engine speed and deft maneuvering to take on worse conditions, Goober was confident that as long as he stayed quartering into the waves and didn't broach, he could close that distance to get back to the straits. Groovy was not so confidant. He began to panic almost immediately. He was yelling and waving his arms, attempting to give the pilot instructions by verbal and non-verbal means.

Fortunately, Goober was used to ignoring him. Just to make the cheese more binding, the throttle return spring on the engine was heavier than it should have been. This meant that as soon as one backed off a little on the throttle, the engine dropped back almost to idle. When fighting heavy seas, it is important to keep an effective throttle. If not, one loses control of the ability to steer, and before you know it you are running before the waves. Running before the waves would not be an especially big problem on open water, but here it would fetch them up on the middle reefs and wreck the boat. They would be in 50-degree water and unlikely to do well at all.

Around the corner they headed and almost right away were slammed hard between the wave tops. This was a jolt that could loosen the rivets on a battleship, and Groovy began going nuts. Goober righted his course and began going faster along the wave tops, cutting that distance to the channel entry spot. It took a firm grip on the throttle with his right hand and a firm grip on the wheel with his left as he gauged the next couple of waves. You can't do much about the wave you're on, but you may be able to react to the next one or two.

Waves of a certain size are not uniform. While they were looking at 10- to 12-footers for the most part, on occasion these waves would almost cancel each other, and a fairly flat spell would appear. This was a chance to accelerate and make some headway. Also, the converse was true: the waves would occasionally nearly double in size.

Waves that are almost as high as the boat is long are a bad thing. This happened again, and they slammed down hard after taking a breaker over the bow. Groovy was now in total panic mode, yelling, waving, and generally being a pain.

Then Goober had an idea. Since the GPS uses a liquid crystal display, it is hard to read it in the sunshine. Moreover, he was occupied with the oncoming waves, the wheel, and the throttle. There was no rain but enough spray to obscure the windshield. He yelled at Groovy to read off the numbers on the GPS.

The readings told of the diminishing distance to the buoy. This kept Traynor busy as well as encouraging both of them that progress was being made. As they made way, Goober turned a little to the south to take on the wave crests and a little to the west in the troughs. Groovy called off the hundredths to go: 65, 57, 52, 45, and on. They had to come within 12 one-hundredths to be able to turn up-channel on the straits. If not, they'd be too far east to find the middle of the channel.

They made it without any further trouble or mishap. Heading up the Strait, Goober handed the wheel to Groovy and shook the tension out of both his arms. That invisible hand pushed them toward home. They gained speed and moved from waves to current as their influencing force. They made it around the corner with the knowledge that it could have been a whole lot worse.

A few days later, heading up to hunt muskies again, Goober asked Groovy, "How scared were you the other day?"

"On a scale of one to ten?"

"Yeah."

"About an eleven and a half."

The day after coming around the corner, Loonch did it by himself. It was challenging, with 5- to 8-footers, but he was confident. It was routine.

Chapter Three

GIRTHRA GOES OVER MUSKY FALLS

One-third of musky men are smashed up in cars, die in their beds, are on lawnmowers that overturn, or succumb while shoveling snow. Another two-thirds give up musky fishing, move to Florida, and spend their remaining time hunting for an early-bird special. A rare few go out doing what they love, fishing.

Lucky Leskowski died of hypothermia after falling overboard; his son could not haul him back aboard. A tragedy. Musky men go out alone in weather when the water is too cold. They shouldn't do so, but they do it anyway. A problem with being out alone is a truly trophy fish is darn near impossible to land on one's own.

Despite the danger of even an inordinately calm day in November on the Upper Lake, Goober was convinced that there were big muskies along the Canadian shore, not a lot of muskies, but some. The bass and walleyes stacked up along the points on that shore on the western edges of the southerly jutting points. Some of these points, like Whiteman and Windjammer, were obvious but several more were submerged and invisible above water.

An old bass-fishing geezer, Dan Prestle, whom Melvin, "Goober" Loonch talked with often, had sworn for years that a giant musky inhabited Windjammer point. Prestle claimed that the muskies would swallow the bass on their way to being reeled in. Without even getting hooked, they would spit the bass out at boatside and swim away. On rare occasions, they would get hooked on the relatively tiny bass hook, and Dan would cut his line and retie.

He liked to tell Loonch that he killed all these muskies, which he may have done in the old days. Dan had been on the river for 70 years. These days, he let the muskies go and told Goober he killed them just to bust his chops.

Goober's problem was that nobody shared his itch to probe the Canadian points. Coupled with that problem, those points were rough as a cob in the west winds of November.

Loonch was out alone on Thanksgiving morning, the weather was very calm, and he resisted the desire to fish the Pantherville Harbor. Whiteman point, 7 miles from the head of the straits, was too far. He decided to start at Windjammer Point, 4.5 miles west. The Upper Lake is huge from the standpoint of a musky hunter, who generally likes short runs of a mile or less, pounded over and over.

When the open lake is fished, it seems hopeless. musky hunters are tenacious, but, it is to be hoped, they are not foolhardy. Fishing the open lake seems foolhardy.

Goober had plotted three points with his GPS during some calm summer days: Windjammer Point, Forbidden Point, and Backhand Point. These points got smaller and less obvious as one moved east toward the straits. They were each loaded with smallmouth bass. Parts of Forbidden Point were even off limits to fishing altogether because the bass spawned there so heavily. Each point degraded as it poked south into the lake, and it was the structure at the ends of the points that Loonch fished. The structure becomes a boulder field and then just a pile of rocks as it degrades. Smallmouth bass love rocks because they turn the crawfish out from under them. The full moon turns on the crawfish as well as the bass. Goober wasn't sure that crawfish were doing anything in November, but the bass reacted to the plenilune nevertheless. The muskies, in turn, reacted to the bass.

At Windjammer point, Goober was able to fish southward down the west side and then, after rounding the tip of the point, northward up its east side. He would then cross the base of the point and repeat the maneuver in reverse. He trolled a baby bass depth raider just above the rocks on one rod and a chartreuse-and-gold perch bait ticking bottom on the other rod. If he had another licensed angler on the boat, he would have used a plow to crash bottom and suspended something else high in the water above it to look for cruising muskies. It is frustrating to crash bottom alone, as hang-ups will occur and nobody likes to lose lures.

Loonch ran this Windjammer run seven times. He caught nothing but some floating moss, the famous Cleland eels that form a ribbon on the leader swivel. He sat down to eat a sandwich and check his leaders as he drifted toward Forbidden Point.

Forbidden Point, invisible from the surface, is not long enough to run by going north to south. He used an oval run wherein he crossed the point repeatedly in a loop or a figure-eight alternately. The boys called these loopy runs "Ceremonial 88s." He pounded the Forbidden Zone 12 times. He caught no fish.

Five hours had elapsed. Goober headed for Backhand Point. Also underwater, Backhand was so short that Loonch's run was a continuous loop, always turning. This was the best point for bass. They were always concentrated on the same spot. While bass fishing at Backhand is hot, musky fishing there provides plenty of time for contemplation and watching the sky. Today, therefore, was a typical day of musky fishing at Backhand Point.

No matter how many times one goes out, the sky and water and weather always combine in different ways. This day, as Goober began his pounding of Backhand Point, he noticed a great cloud bank rolling toward him from Canada to the Northwest. The storms of the Upper Lake had once been compared to the Bull of Heaven charging and crashing across the sky. Goober kept checking that direction and began to listen for the telltale sound of thunder. Thunder and lightning would put an end to musky fishing. Thunder in November in northern latitudes is rare but not unheard of.

A few years previously, thunder snow had occurred in Pantherville during Thanksgiving week. The weatherman had said on the radio that thundersnow wouldn't happen more than once in one's lifetime. It not only took place all day that day but was back one week later. That Thanksgiving week storm had set up over Pantherville in a snow band and dropped snow at a rate of 7 inches per hour for 4 hours. The schools had tried to send the kids home on buses in the middle of the storm, and everyone became stuck. The streets were filled with abandoned cars. People got stranded in their cars. The buses blocked the roads. The plows couldn't clear the roads because of all the derelict vehicles.

Typical of Pantherville, the people pitched in to help each other. Stranded motorists were taken into homes. The school children were taken off the buses and brought into restaurants and businesses. Those who stayed in their vehicles all night were okay because the temperature didn't get really cold and there was no wind. Wind would have pushed the snow band away. It was days later when the roads could be cleared and the abandoned cars recovered.

Thoughts of such an early season storm began to intrude on the meditation Loonch practiced as he musky fished.

Backhand Point comes up a little higher than the points to the west. It reaches 21 feet in some places as opposed to the 24 feet of Windjammer Point. Goober had begun to get rips, line being pulled out against the drag, from his deeper-diving perch bait. He brought that lure in a little to keep it ticking bottom but without getting snagged.

Loonch was heading in a south-southeasterly direction, facing the Pantherville skyline and glancing toward the cloud bank scudding across the Southtowns, when he heard a constant rip. The line was screaming from the drag on one of his reels.

A constant clicking of the reel is usually interpreted as a snag. Fish, even very big fish, usually pause while pulling against the drag. They probably shake their head when they feel they have been hooked. Goober instinctively turned to the port side, where his deep diver had been catching bottom, but he was surprised to see that it wasn't the reel giving out line.

His depth raider rig was still screaming as he dashed to strike the rod without shifting the boat to neutral. Thumbing the reel and yanking back on the rod, he felt a tremendous pull. It was not a snag. Goober had caught the bottom often, as well as several pipelines, bridge abutments, and sunken ships. He knew the difference between a fish and a snag. This didn't peel off line like a thumb-burning snag, but it was a big enough fish that his thumb barely slowed it down.

"This is a big fish!" he said aloud to himself. The rod tip was up, and his thumb was slowing the reel, but he didn't want to tighten the drag too much and let the fish break something. He had 50-pound-test line, 120-pound-test leader, and 300-pound-test swivel and split rings. However, he had seen muskies break lures and straighten hooks. In fact, Goober no longer considered using wooden lures because they had come back in pieces too many times.

The boat was still going forward slowly toward the head of the straits. Normally, he would just step to the throttle and drop the engine into neutral, but he had to be comfortable that it was not necessary for him to give the fish 100 percent of his attention. The reel kept screaming, and more line went out.

"I can't expect this fish to pull a 6,000-pound boat," he thought as he eased himself toward the throttle. Line burned off under his thumb. He reached inside the flap at the back of his winter cover and groped for the throttle. Out of the corner of his eye, he saw a huge black cloud looming. It was then that he heard a thunder clap. He loosened his grip on the reel, and line began screaming out again. The thunder rolled over him down the straits. He dropped the throttle to neutral. It began to snow, hard.

The boat was drifting rapidly downstream through the straits when he returned to the fish. His line counter was at 337 feet; it had started at 95. Goober still had the problem of the second rod's lure that would float up to the surface and possibly tangle with the monster fish. He was also wondering if maybe he had hooked a sturgeon. They could grow to over a hundred pounds. Loonch began gaining line and looking for an opportunity to pull in that second rod.

He was now in snow so heavy that he couldn't see the front of his boat. The snow was building up on the deck and cockpit. When would it overbalance the boat? He had heard about boats in Alaska getting so heavy with ice that they turned turtle.

He had begun gaining line back. Despite the snow and zero visibility, Goober felt better about his situation. He looked at the line counter, now at 301. There were still problems. His VHF radio had died a few days earlier, but he did have a portable for backup. He had a cell phone. He continued to pump and reel; 257 feet and gaining.

The current and the storm were sweeping him along at what he would have ordinarily considered an impossible speed. When one cannot see anything on shore and only feels the wind, sees the choppy waves, and hears the rushing sound, it is very scary.

"Can snow pile up when it is driven sideways by the wind? Yes!

"How close am I to the Friendship Bridge? Surely, I'll see that.

"When is this fish going to tangle my second line? I better get that in now."

These thoughts were churning through Goober's mind. He put the rod in a holder, upright to keep tension on it, and jumped to grab the second rod. The rod with the fish started screaming again. He jumped back and thumbed the reel once again.

He stopped the line going out: 301 feet and stable. After he got his fish under control, Goober stepped to the console and picked up his portable VHF. He thought about getting on the musky channel and seeing if anyone else was out. He turned the radio on; it was dead—batteries gone. Had he left it on the last time out?

He went back to gaining line: 289 and closing. Then, the whooshing sound made by the storm and current changed slightly. He looked up, then he turned to look downstream.

A huge bridge piling loomed dead ahead. It was barely visible through the snow, but he heard a truck's air horn on the bridge. Rod in his right hand, he reached for the throttle to gun the engine away from the bridge. He slammed the handle forward so hard that the engine stalled. No time was left to start the boat.

Sure to hit the abutment, he swallowed hard and thought of the life jacket he did not have on. At the last second, the push of current around the prow of the bridge piling swept his boat down the side of the huge stone mass, just inches from the boat being raked by the stone. The second rod was snapped in half by the bridge, and the line went all wobbly behind it. At the downstream end of the piling, the boat swirled into a back flow. The broken rod started screaming line as the lure must have caught the bridge.

All this happened with Goober just staring and holding the rod with the fish. The second rod stopped pulling drag, and *Booster* was rushing downstream again. There was zero visibility and plenty of snow. The water below that bridge is some of the fastest current on the Upper Straits. Goober was again flying along. He began gaining line again: 240 feet and closing.

There was another bridge coming up, but below that was a breakwall, behind which the water would flow backwards. He could get out of the current once he made it there—*if* he could only start his boat and pull east a few hundred feet.

Goober thought he should gain as much line as possible between the bridges. He began reeling like a maniac, trying to shorten up his line. At one point, while resting his arms, the clouds to the west cleared, and he saw Iggy casting away on his favorite drift. Iggy was in sunlight, but Goober was still in the darkness of the snow band.

"My cell phone! I'll call him," he thought, but then realized he couldn't remember Igg's number. He went back to his line, now down to 120 feet, nearly at the length it had started peeling off from up on Backhand Point. A muffled, rattling noise rose behind him, and he turned to see the railroad bridge looming. This time, the boat split the uprights between two abutments.

Goober returned to his line and began hauling hard on the fish he had on. Up until now, he'd gained line only when the fish volunteered to swim toward the boat. Now he had a fight on his hands, and what a fight it was! He pumped the rod and reeled up on each down-stroke, gaining only a few feet each time.

The mind plays tricks on one when one is alone. It is reassuring to have someone to talk to, even if it is a person devoid of ideas. When one is alone and considering options and the approval or disagreement of a companion is therefore lacking, the choices can roll around in the mind without resolution. That is what happened to Goober as he thought about the snow building up on the canvas top and decks of the *Booster*.

The snow band had picked up intensity and was directly overhead as he plowed along under the second bridge. He didn't carry anything like a snow shovel in his boat. A boat hook would be useless for pushing snow. He didn't even have a mop or brush for cleaning the boat; both were back at the boathouse. The roiling ideas in his brain and a growing seed of panic combined to make him almost immobile. He had even stopped reeling. The fish was swimming along with the boat scudding downstream. The snow was building up. He knew he had to start the stalled engine if he was to duck behind the breakwall.

Goober couldn't see beyond his boat. His radios were both down. He couldn't settle on a course of action. "Do something, even if it's wrong," was the thought that took over. He set his rod in its holder and scooted into the driver's seat. He would start the motor. Getting behind the breakwall might lose the fish but would solve the other problems, he reasoned.

He advanced the throttle in neutral and turned the key. The engine cranked and sputtered and started. At that point, one must drop the shifter back into neutral and shift smoothly into forward to proceed. Any attempt at doing this that was done too abruptly could stall the engine. Goober knew that repeated stalls would flood the engine, and it would require a wait of 10 or more minutes to start.

Loonch's panic caused him to jerk the shifter into forward too fast. The engine stalled. He re-started and tried again. He stalled again. He looked about and could not tell where he was. The reel started giving out line slowly: *click, click, click*. He tried the engine again. Now, it would not start at all. Flooded.

"The kicker!" He thought of his trolling motor, which could still save the day. The trolling motor was a four-stroke outboard that was so quiet that one couldn't hear it start in any kind of wind. The wind was rushing past like an open car window at 55 mph.

Then, *BANG*, the boat hit something. Goober looked up to see a green buoy as the boat rolled down its east side. He knew he was well past the breakwall now. The tiny kicker would take forever to get there, going against both the current and the wind.

"Time for plan B," he thought. *Click, click, click.* "What the heck *is* plan B?" Loonch grabbed the rod. He didn't know much, but he knew how to catch a musky—or so he thought.

The fish had only taken out 21 more feet of line, and Goober started bringing it in from 120 feet. The fish came right toward the boat. It was either exhausted or swimming faster than he could reel. Exhausted would mean death for Girthra. Goober was now convinced that he had the giant she-musky of myth on his line. He couldn't be the man who killed Girthra. After all his cockiness and bragging, he was in an impossible position.

He continued to gain line. Seventy-six feet; Lou Groza's number. The snow was building up on the top—the most dangerous place. Sixty-three feet; Fuzzy Thurston's number. Try the cell phone. The clouds to the east parted, and he saw a boat heading for the town launch site.

It was JohnJohn and Clem. Maybe they'd see him. He waved. They were in sunshine. He was in the dark snow cloud. He glanced over. Clem was facing to the rear. They were running from the weather. Clem appeared to be leaning over to see behind the boat past JohnJohn. He said something. JohnJohn turned around, looked, shook his head, and headed in to the boat launch.

"They didn't see me!" Goober thought.

Goober was running out of options. He looked over the side to see if the buoy had done much damage. It appeared to be just a streak of green paint. But, there were many buoys ahead even though the straits were wide. He didn't want to think about contending with another one while adrift.

The only number he could think of to call with his cell phone was Snooky's. He dialed it with one hand and held his rod tip high with the other while jamming the rod into his belt.

He was becoming disoriented. He could see so little—just the boat and an occasional glimpse of a member of the Straits Musky Club who couldn't help him. It was like the moment before sleep when dreaming has started and the world closes around one like a cotton cocoon. It was a state that could lead to pleasant dreams or nightmares or death.

He finished punching in Snooky's number, got an answering machine, and said, "I'm in the river, I have a giant fish, I'm in trouble."

BANG! The cell phone flew from his hand, separated itself from its battery, and slid into the scupper that was 7 inches deep in slush. The boat had hit another buoy, this time on the east side. A nun had scraped down the starboard side. Communication was gone. The engine wouldn't start. What about the anchor?

"Catch the fish first, then anchor the boat, and work on the anchor rope," Goober stated his plan to himself.

The fish was fighting again. Slowly, Goober gained line. Fifty-one feet; Dick Butkus's number. The snow began to let up. He slipped past the power plant. He smelled the coal smoke brought low by the weather. Forty-four feet; Ernie Davis's number. The straits turned a corner here and flattened out. The current slowed down a little but, but Goober knew he would soon drift into the fastest-moving part of the main current.

It was a forlorn hope to wish he would slide over into some

flat spot where he'd be able to calm down his mind and the things happening to him. Thirty-two feet; Jimmy Brown's number and O.J.'s and a million other guys'. Goober had a mile before the next bridge. He hoped to get Girthra up to the boat, released, and get to work on what could be done with the boat by then. He pumped hard and reeled hard a few times. Twenty feet; his lucky number. He should be able to see something of the fish by now.

The snow had closed in again after having been driven off by the power plant's emissions. He pumped and reeled three more times. Twelve feet; he thought he saw a fin break the surface. Keep reeling.

Seven feet, and there loomed a shape huge, brownish, long. "It can't be *that* big!" he told himself.

The fish began to take line. Seeing the size of it, Goober backed the drag off to let her have line while he dashed for the big musky net. He grabbed a couple of bungee cords so the fish wouldn't take net and all to Davy Jones' locker.

The boat was slowing some, and the fish, looking 10 feet long, was placidly swimming alongside, casting an inquiring eye at the boat. Loonch cranked it in to 3 feet and placed the rod in the holder that was farthest forward. The fish was hooked on the first of three treble hooks, with the other two hanging outside her mouth on the side nearest the boat.

Seeing this, Goober knew he needed to net her without hooking those trebles so he could get most of her into the net before the hooks tangled the mesh. Her head was as big as a basketball. She was long, long, long. He put the reel on free spool and scooped the net toward her. Surprisingly, she swam right into the basket. Goober got her tail inside, grabbed his bungees, and secured the net to the boat so he could work with both his hands.

"Get a measurement!" he thought.

The measuring stick was 60 inches long, and when he floated it beside the fish, it was at least 10 inches too short. Even then, the fish was curved slightly to fit in the net.

"This fish is over 6 feet long!" He said aloud. "I gotta get a photograph," Goober thought. With the fish alongside, he snapped two shots with the disposable camera he had on board.

Then the trouble began.

With the fish in the water and in the net, Goober reached down with his long-nosed pliers to remove the hook from the corner of her mouth. She saw the pliers coming and took one shake and flipped the last treble hook right into the wrist cuff of Goober's Straits Musky Club wind shirt. This was a brand new item of clothing and well made to be rip-proof.

The hooks were through the shirt, a long-sleeved under shirt, and into his right wrist. Being right-handed, Goober had reached down to unhook the fish with that hand. Now he had to extricate himself with his off-hand. He switched the pliers to his left and reached for the hook in his wrist.

Girthra gave another shake and buried the middle treble hook in his right hand, just below his little finger. He was bleeding a little now. He wondered if he could reach his hook cutters. Musky men carry heavy duty hook cutters—the best ones are made in Germany—to keep from having the fish out of water for long. Goober's were on a lanyard attached to the center of the board in the back of his boat.

He dropped the pliers inside the boat and twisted around to reach left-handed for the cutters. His right hand was firmly attached to the fish that now began to swim away inside the net. The boat had 20 inches of freeboard and was 7 feet wide. He stretched all the way out, and was still 6 inches from the cutters.

Girthra pulled again, and he was even farther away. He tried to pull her in and lift her enough to stretch back for the cutters. Goober could feel the treble hooks lodge deeper into his wrist and hand. She was too heavy and too lively.

Maybe he could pull her into the boat with both hands and then get the cutters. He tried. She was too big and heavy and slippery and slimy. He couldn't do anything with her. He tried to relax—no mean feat with his arm hooked in two places and his body turned inside out over the gunwale.

He looked up to see the Big Island Bridge overhead. He heard the melting snow runoff from it pelting his boat. Was that the first or the second bridge? Was he on his way over the cascade? Time for action.

Goober looked back at the cutters and saw the Bogagrip sitting on the engine cover. He now had a plan.

He pulled Girthra as close as he could. His wrist was really starting to hurt, now that the original adrenaline rush had worn off. He stretched backward as if crucified and got his left hand on the Bogagrip. With a lunge, he was able to grab the lanyard on his third try. He pulled, and the cutters rattled across the engine cover and deck. He reeled them up with the lanyard to his left hand.

It would be logical to cut the hook in the fish's mouth first and then the ones in his hand and wrist. But the fish's hook was blocked by his right hand, which lay fast along her jaw. The closest hook was under two layers of clothing and had to be cut from the far side.

Loonch thought, "If only I'd been wearing my usual rags instead of this GoreTex Straits Musky Club shirt, I could just rip away the fabric." His left hand, being non-dominant, was beginning to cramp up as he wrestled with this problem.

His body was now on the gunwale full length, with his left leg hanging over the side. He managed to cut the hook in his hand and reached under his cuffs for the one in his wrist. Just as he got the cutters around that hook shank and snipped, Girthra gave a tremendous shake of her head. She threw her hook right out of her mouth and into the net. She was now unhooked but still in the net.

Goober was unhooked in his arm, but his cuff was still caught and attached to the net. Also, Girthra's head-shake had pulled him almost out of the boat, with only his right leg still inside the gunwale.

He let go of the hook cutters. They snapped back on the lanyard and smacked him above the right eye. He squinted and felt dizzy. When he opened his eyes, he saw a blood trail drifting out behind the boat.

The fish was unhooked and placidly swimming beside the boat. She was in the net still but in no danger. Goober's troubles were with himself.

He had parts of two treble hooks in his right hand. His clothes were stuck in the net, one hook in his cuff, and two in the net. He was bleeding over his right eye and couldn't keep that eye open. He was freezing. His one free hand, the left, was stiff and arthritic and only marginally useful in the best of times. These, most assuredly, were not the best of times.

Loonch was hanging out over the gunwale and almost in the water. He realized at this moment that he couldn't move his right leg back into the boat. The bottom of his pants had become entwined in the rear cleat on the boat. Here he was, wearing his usual rags, and a hole in the hem of his insulated pants had caught on the cleat. Though he jerked his leg back, forward, around and back, in all directions, it was held fast. Without that right leg in the boat, he couldn't crawl back inside.

Goober switched his attention to getting his arm and himself unhooked from the net. He remembered his father's knife, one that he always carried while fishing. He struggled to reach it in his right pants pocket with his left hand. This was a stretching, cramping, exercise not made easier by being a fat tub who couldn't reach across his belly.

He stretched and grunted and reached and finally got the blade into the left hand. Now he had to put it in his right hand to open the blade with his left. This knife was an old fashioned one that, luckily, did not have a locking blade. He took the blade, not a very sharp one, in his left hand.

With his hand cramping and his grip slipping, he started to cut down through the GoreTex cuff. He had to free the lure from his clothes so he could use two hands to pull himself back into the boat. He sliced, cut, and got through some layers of clothing. Suddenly, blood started gushing.

"Oh my God, I've slashed my own wrist! I've got to cut up to not make this worse!"

The waves were slapping at him as the boat drifted, and the flowing blood was immediately washing away. He could only see his work with his one unswollen eye. He was cold. He was very, very, cold.

Melvin tried to make himself calm. He had to gather the strength to do what he needed to do. He reached the knife blade up inside the cuff and gripped it as tightly as he could.

Goober didn't realize that he had passed beneath the North Big Island Bridge, slid across the top of the big island, and entered Canadian waters. He had also crossed the dead line where boats should turn back to avoid being swept over the cascade.

He tried to concentrate through a fog of pain, cold, blindness, and cramping. He got his knife into position under the cuff of his Straits Musky Club wind shirt.

BANG! The boat had hit bottom and turned its bow downriver, wedging in some rocks. The net caught and turned inside out, releasing Girthra. With the impact of the grounding, Goober's knife pulled suddenly through the fabric and jammed its full 5 inches into his neck. Another gush of blood turned the river red.

He watched Girthra rocket out of the net and, boosted by the current, head straight over the cascades. The snowstorm, that Bull of Heaven, followed Girthra toward the falls. Goober was in bright sunshine. He felt the slight heat on his cold, cold, body. He gathered his strength and tried to flip himself into the boat. He only succeeded halfway. He got his left arm into the boat but his right arm was still tangled in the net by his shirt sleeve.

He lay there with his back along the gunwale, his arms outstretched, his feet tangled in the cleat on the back of the boat and the sun shining down on him. He reached his arm to pull the knife from his neck but stopped himself, thinking he would just bleed more with the blade removed.

The sun slipped behind a cloud. The world turned red, then blue, then black, then white. Melvin Loonch tried a few more times to flip himself into the boat then lost consciousness.

Girthra had broken free at the brink of the cascades. She'd gone over while Goober was beaten like a rag doll against the boat that was aground 66 feet above the cascades.

The Cascades Parks Police later removed him after a call from the United States Coast Guard. They had gotten a call from the New York State Department of Environmental Conservation. They had gotten a call from Snooky when he checked his messages.

The officers said Loonch looked like a windsock having been left out through several Pantherville winters. He'd been beaten against the side of the *Booster* as he bled out. The officers recovered the camera, and the photos of Girthra were eventually developed. That might have been a world record musky. She had fulfilled Musky Bill's last saying, "Whatever you've got, there's a musky that can defeat it."

THE DEATH OF DREAMING

Trout, salmon, trout: greasy, oily, delicious trout. Look at those fat trout. And they croak when crunched. Just swimming by, waiting for me to eat: trout.

Finny Minny jerked himself up out of a troubled sleep. He looked at his legs with the sheet and blanket wrapped around and around his right leg. He remembered the seven scenes that had been coursing through his dream, faster and faster, like a flipchart out of control. A musky boat at the dock, a looming reef, a snow-filled cloud chasing him downstream, a 20-foot wave crashing over the top of his boat, a giant musky at boatside, waiting to be netted, a summer evening with his daughter catching three muskies on four runs, a treble hook piercing his wrist. Finn's dreams had been so intense since he had forsworn his Schnapps that he often dreamed during the day. Simply by putting his eyes out of focus or closing them he could dream. This last dream had been his most intense of all.

Afterword

Was this meant to be a totalizing meta-narrative of musky lore? No. I hope this book showed how an insecure, iconoclastic, know-nothing like Goober, caught up in politics and personality, missed the mark for years in absorbing the knowledge needed to catch muskies efficiently.

How he finally found the meaning of the sayings of Musky Bill should have made you smile, and, occasionally, smack your forehead with the heel of your hand as you recognized yourself or someone you knew.

While taken from reality, none of these people are real. Several were dissected into two or more parts to show multiple aspects of personality.

There are not two sides to every question; there are more like 17 sides.

Read this for laughs; read it for lore. For Girthra's sake, don't take it seriously.

Richard A. Minich
July 2004

Handy Order Form

Postal orders: All Esox Publications
P.O. Box 493
East Aurora, New York 14052

Fax orders: 716-655-2621
Phone Orders: 716-655-2621
email orders: clelandeel@mindspring.com
website: AllEsoxPublications.com

Please send the following materials.
I understand that I may return any of them for a full refund, for any reason, no questions asked:

_____

_____

_____

Please send more information on publications:
Yes_____No_____

Name: _____

Address: _____

City:_____

State/Prov: _____Zip/Postal Code_____

Sales Tax: NYS residents add 8.25%

Shipping U.S $2.00 (Can $3.00) for first item; $1.00 (Can $1.50) each add'l item

Payment: Check____ Credit Card: Visa____Mastercard____

Card Number: _____

Name: _____

Exp. Date:_____
Signature: _____

In Case you missed it...

An excerpt from

The Accidental Musky

Published by All Esox Publications

ISBN 0-9758728-4-2

Musky Lore

The Muskellunge is a North American phenomenon and has a much smaller natural range than the Northern Pike. It can't spawn or even survive in water too warm or too cold. The Canadian Shield and the Great Lakes contiguous areas are all there is, though, it has been introduced into a much wider area.

The oral traditions of the Native American Tribes around the Great Lakes speak of the Muskellunge with awe and dread. While supplying a large meal when captured, they also must have wreaked havoc on fish traps and scared off the smaller species at least temporarily.

When Europeans began referring to the Musky in the 17th century it was the Jesuit diaries that transcribed the folk tradition of the Native Americans. From these early references tales still exist of, "The Monster of the Manitowish, Old Abe, and Jingle Bells." Some fellows in the Niagara region refer to the she Musky of myth as Girthra.

Do Muskies eat game fish?

The answer to this question is, a little bit. Muskies and Pike both prefer long cylindrical fish. Those shaped like hammer handles are favored. Perch, suckers, redhorse, shiners, dace darters, Cisco, gizzard shad, are typical fare. Cannibalism is common in both species. Yellow perch are game fish and they are the most common Musky prey, but they tend to occur in vast numbers. Suckers rank second in numbers in the Musky diet. Walleyes, while eaten, are uncommon. Bass, bluegill, crappie and rock bass, with their flatter bodies and spiny dorsal fins, are not sought out. Ducklings, Mice, Muskrats, Mules, and Anglers are rare meals indeed. A starving Musky may try to eat anything. I know a fellow who, when pursued for several days by the Viet Cong, ate a tarantula in one bite. He has not eaten one since.

Coming June 2005

All Esox Publications Proudly Presents

A preview of

Becoming A Musky Hunter

Richard A. Minich

Watch for it

How Muskies are Caught by Accident

I was reeling in the inside rod to clean weeds when the drag on the outside one went crazy. It was screaming steadily like a snag. I quickly placed one rod in the holder and grabbed for the second. With line peeling off, I lifted and felt for resistance. It was a fish, and a big one too! I was fishing for bass, but I obviously had something bigger than a bass. It was a musky.

The same rod, reel, and lure that is used for very gratifying smallmouth bass will bring a bite from the occasional accidental musky. I was using a Yo-Zuri crystal minnow less than five inches long. That lure had caught six bass from 15 to 19 inches. Now it had a 46 inch musky that weighed at least twenty pounds.

To get her in, unhooked, and released I had to count on my rod to do the work, and my arms too. The twelve-pound test line was overmatched and, fishing for bass, I had no leader on the business end of the line.

I turned the boat away from shore, since this fight was going to take a few minutes. I didn't want to be up against the riprap when the critical moment came. I pumped and reeled and got her close but she wouldn't leave the bottom. Muskies will often jump and fight on the surface, but when caught on lightweight gear, they don't seem to feel the pull and fight back by hunkering down and staying in place. Eventually, I got her to come up and saw what I had. She was a beauty, with a big head and the typical greenish brown color. That five-inch lure was completely inside her mouth.

Now, I had to land her. Luckily, I am a musky specialist and have all the gear on my boat, even when I'm fishing for bass or walleye. I had the big net, hook cutters, jaw spreaders, and long needle nose pliers, but the light line and lack of a leader, still put Mrs. Musky in danger of swimming away with a crankbait embedded in her lips. I had another problem, though. It was an outstanding early season afternoon for boating and the boat wakes of the happy cruisers had pushed me into the bank. I had to head back out into the open water before I could unhook her safely.

I switched out of neutral, loosened the drag, and headed out for mid-channel. The drag screamed again and she ended up sixty feet behind me when I shifted back into neutral. On the surface now, she knew she was hooked and put up a scrap. I had to catch her twice. The second time she came alongside the boat she only had one treble hook left in her mouth. I corralled her alongside in the big net and reached down with my long needle nose pliers to remove that last hook. Just as I pulled it away, the line broke just above the snap swivel. She had abraded the line when the lure was all the way in her mouth. I laid my floating measuring stick alongside her and got the vital data. With my right hand on her tail I gently tried to turn her upside down. She didn't want any of that and flipped back over, gave a twitch of her powerful tail, and she was gone in a second.

Muskies are caught this way often around my home waters and they are thrilling on light tackle. It is not the best way to musky fish, however. As the snap of that line shows, it is too easy for the big lunge to get away with a mouthful of hooks. Odds are 4 to 1 or better that she would never get those hooks out of her mouth. The hooks don't dissolve, rust out or magically disappear before she dies. Any attempt to corral her by pulling on the line, a way to position a musky when you have a heavy leader to pull her with, would have snapped that line.

From the forthcoming book, *Becoming a Musky Hunter* by Richard A. Minich

Richard A. Minich, the author of The Accidental Musky *and* The Quest for Girthra, *is a member of Muskies Inc., Muskies Canada Inc., and the Niagara Musky Association. He divides his time among the three Rs: readin', ritin' and reelin' in muskies.*

Handy Order Form

Postal orders: All Esox Publications
P.O. Box 493
East Aurora, New York 14052

Fax orders: 716-655-2621
Phone Orders: 716-655-2621
email orders: clelandeel@mindspring.com
website: AllEsoxPublications.com

Please send the following materials.

I understand that I may return any of them for a full refund, for any reason, no questions asked:

_____

_____

_____

Please send more information on publications:
Yes_____No_____

Name: _____

Address: _____

City:_____

State/Prov: _____Zip/Postal Code_____

Sales Tax: NYS residents add 8.25%

Shipping U.S $2.00 (Can $3.00) for first item; $1.00 (Can $1.50) each add'l item

Payment: Check____ Credit Card: Visa____Mastercard____

Card Number: _____

Name: _____

Exp. Date:_____

Signature: _____